SARATOGA

For Kathy and Ken

SARATOGA

TURNING POINT IN THE

AMERICAN REVOLUTION

MARTHA BYRD

AUERBACH.
publishers

philadelphia
new york
london

Copyright © AUERBACH Publishers Inc. 1973

Published simultaneously in United Kingdom by AUERBACH Publishers Inc., Wallington, Surrey, England.

Library of Congress Catalog Card Number: 72-81815
International Standard Book Number: 0-87769-143-6

First Printing

Printed in the United States of America

Library of Congress Cataloging in Publication Data

Byrd, Martha, 1930-
    Saratoga; turning point in the American Revolution

(Great events in world history)
    SUMMARY: Describes the immediate causes, events, and aftermath of the Saratoga campaign, a series of encounters which marked a turning point in the Revolutionary War in favor of the rebel colonists.
    Bibliography: p.
    1. Saratoga, Campaign, 1777. 2. Burgoyne's Invasion, 1777. 3. Schuylerville, N. Y.--History. [1. Saratoga Campaign, 1777. 2. Burgoyne's Invasion 1777. 3. United States--History--Revolution] I. Title.
E241.S2B97   973.3'33   72-81815
ISBN 0-87769-143-6

Contents

List of Illustrations

SARATOGA

1. Why at Saratoga?

It is October 17, 1777. The forests around Saratoga, on the upper Hudson River, are a blaze of autumn color. On the high ground west of the river, 5,000 of His Majesty's soldiers stand behind fortified positions to which a dismal retreat has just brought them. Their once-brilliant uniforms are shabby; their once-proud spirit is subdued. In the meadows and woods surrounding them, and on the cliffs overlooking them from across the river, a tatterdemalion army of Americans, three times their number, waits and watches.

James Wilkinson, a twenty-year-old American colonel, rides into the British camp. Presently he rides out again, accompanied by Lieutenant General John Burgoyne and other British officers. The party makes its way the short distance to the American camp, where they are met by Major General Horatio Gates. The American general wears "a plain blue frock," the British general a "rich royal uniform." The boy colonel speaks their names in introduction. With courtly grace, General Burgoyne raises his hat and says, "The fortune of war, General Gates, has made me your prisoner."

His conqueror replies with equal formality, "I shall always be ready to bear testimony that it has not been through any fault of your excellency."[1]

With dignity and restraint, General Gates and his American Army accepted the British surrender at Saratoga. The event formally ended the Saratoga campaign of 1777 and marked the first large-scale success for colonial arms in the American Revolution. Its aftermath shaped the nature and eventual outcome of that long struggle, for American victory at Saratoga gave hope to the American cause and forced Britain to change her strategy in the war. Even more important, however, it encouraged France to make an open alliance with the Americans—an alliance that proved crucial to American victory in the Revolution. Because it precipitated that alliance, the Saratoga campaign is called the turning point of the American Revolution.

To appreciate the Saratoga campaign, it is necessary to begin with the events of the preceding years, for Saratoga was not a single great battle, but rather the climactic finale to a three-year struggle for a strategic military position—the Hudson-St. Lawrence waterway.

Once the political differences between the colonists and their mother country erupted in open conflict, each side had to determine how it could win a military victory. For the first three years of the Revolution, both British and American strategy was based on gaining control of the vital waterway linking New York and Canada—the waterway formed by the Hudson River, Lake George, Lake Champlain, the Richelieu River, and the St. Lawrence River.

Why did both the British and the Americans consider the Hudson-St. Lawrence waterway important enough to fight for? What would be gained by holding it?

Bodies of water have played a major role in history. This role has diminished with modern transportation and communication, but in the past waterways separated peoples and cultures and at the same time served as major transportation routes to link those peoples. Two important waterways shaped the pattern of the American Revolution, and both of them also affected the events of Saratoga.

One of these waterways was the Atlantic Ocean, a vast, 3,000-mile-wide expanse of water separating Britain from her American colonies. So great was the distance that sailing ships of the 1770s required about three months to make the round trip between Europe and America. Thus the Atlantic forced the British to wage war at a slow pace and under loose strategic control, because it took so long to transport information, orders, men, and supplies from one continent to the other. In addition, the Atlantic determined that if Britain was to defeat the colonists, she must control the seas to protect her vital transatlantic route. Her navy must be strong, not only in transport vessels, but also in men-of-war. Otherwise the communication-supply lines could be disrupted by aggressive American privateers,[2] and possibly severed entirely if one of Europe's naval powers—such as France—should enter the war against Britain. Therefore, underlying all other activity of the Revolution was the desperate struggle for control of the Atlantic; it was when she lost control at sea that Britain lost the war.

The American colonies themselves were strung out in a narrow band along some 1,500 miles of the Atlantic coastline. The ports—Boston, New York, Philadelphia, and Charleston—were the only real cities. Philadelphia, with a population of 34,000, was the largest. The bulk of the approximately two and one-quarter million colonists lived within 100 to 150 miles of the coast. Albany, 150 miles up the Hudson River and boasting 3,500 persons, was the largest town so far inland. Most of the colonists were concentrated in the coastal area lying between northern Massachusetts and southern Virginia. This more densely populated strip was bisected by the Hudson River, which formed the southern link of the other major waterway that vitally affected the Revolution.

The Hudson-St. Lawrence waterway was an important trade and transportation route in colonial times. The Hudson itself, more than 300 miles long, was navigable by the largest ships of the time, drawing 14 to 20 feet, as far as 100 miles upstream, while the remaining 50 miles to Albany was open to smaller vessels. River craft plied the Hudson above Albany. From Fort Edward, some distance beyond the village of Saratoga, there was a road to connect with Lake George, 12 miles away. Goods shipped up the Hudson had to be transhipped over this short portage to reach Lake George, and there was another short portage at the northern end of Lake George, connecting it to Lake Champlain. From Lake Champlain boats could travel down the Richelieu River to the St. Lawrence, which, like the lower Hudson, could accommodate large oceangoing ships. This water route provided the main transportation route for people and goods moving north-south. Eighteenth-century America had few roads, and the ones it did have were neither hard surfaced nor designed to carry heavy traffic. They were usually little better than dirt tracks that became impassable during bad weather. The Hudson-St. Lawrence waterway served as an 18th-century super-highway, knifing through an essentially roadless wilderness.

The military significance of the Hudson-St. Lawrence route was twofold. Not only did it offer a means of moving the armies, with their cumbersome supplies of stores and artillery, but whichever side controlled the waterway gained strategic and political advantages. If the British could control the Hudson, they could divide the long, narrow strip of coastal America in two, thus isolating New England, where

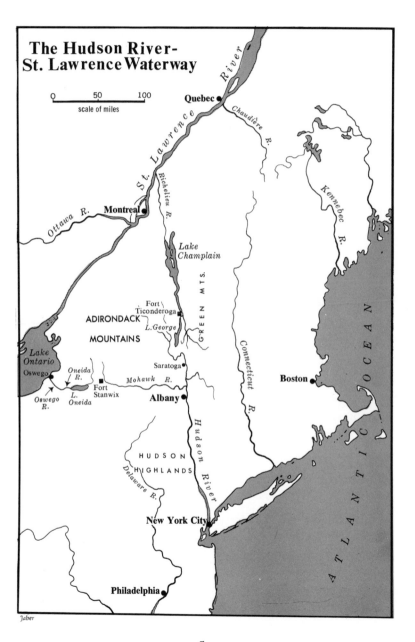

The Hudson River-
St. Lawrence Waterway

0   50   100
scale of miles

Quebec

St. Lawrence

Chaudière R.

Ottawa R.

Montreal

Richelieu R.

Kennebec R.

Lake Champlain

Fort Ticonderoga

ADIRONDACK

GREEN MTS.

L. George

MOUNTAINS

Lake Ontario

Oswego

Oneida R.

Saratoga

Connecticut R.

Boston

Mohawk R.

Fort Stanwix

Oswego R.

L. Oneida

Albany

Hudson River

HUDSON

HIGHLANDS

Delaware R.

A T L A N T I C   O C E A N

New York City

Philadelphia

Jaber

5

rebel resistance was strongest, from the remainder of the colonies. This would not only hurt colonial morale but would make physical cooperation between the two parts of America more difficult. Thus separated, each part would be weakened and could be defeated more readily. Conversely, if the Americans controlled the Hudson, they would benefit from the unity of the colonies.

The Hudson-St. Lawrence route had been militarily important long before 1775. Warring tribes of Indians had used it, and during the French and Indian War (1754-63) the armed forces of France and Britain fought bitterly for its control. Both sides built forts at strategic points. The largest was Fort Carillon, built by the French on a spur of land jutting out into Lake Champlain where its artillery could command both the southern end of Lake Champlain and the northern end of Lake George. Fort Carillon was considered the key to the waterway. When the British captured it from the French in 1759, they renamed it Fort Ticonderoga.

The French and Indian War was the North American portion of the Seven Years' War, in which Britain defeated France. By the terms of the peace settlement, French Canada became a British colony. France, having lost this round in her century-long conflict with Britain, watched subsequent American developments carefully. She would seize any favorable opportunity in the future to embarrass or thwart Britain, and such an opportunity would arise during the American Revolution.

On the eve of the Revolution, Canada was still a predominantly French-speaking, Catholic region. Although this cultural gulf separated Canada from the rest of America, the Canadians had little motivation to join the British in subduing their American neighbors. Neither did the Canadians have real cause for rebellion against Britain, for the British were governing Canada with what was, for the times, an unusually enlightened colonial policy. The Canadians remained essentially neutral in the British-American confrontation.

Britain wanted to keep Canada within the empire; American patriots wanted Canada to join their struggle against Britain. So it was that both sides eyed the Hudson-St. Lawrence waterway—the link between Canada and the Thirteen Colonies. If the British controlled the waterway, they could hold Canada and use it as a base for attacking the rebellious colonists from the north. If the Americans controlled the route, they could protect the rear of their armies from British attack, preserve the link between New England and the southern colonies, and more effectively seek to persuade the Canadians to become the Fourteenth Colony and join forces with them to defeat the British.

Meanwhile, on the eve of the Revolution, the small village of Saratoga, roughly midway between New York and Montreal on the Hudson-St. Lawrence waterway, went about its business without the slightest inkling of the part it would play in the war ahead. Yet Saratoga was the place where the long struggle for the waterway would reach its climax and where the British surrender would be tendered. In later years, the name "Saratoga" was extended to cover the battleground eight miles south where the two most important clashes occurred. That battleground is now preserved within Saratoga National Historical Park, where the events of 1777 may be vividly recalled. The village of Saratoga still exists, but it is now called Schuylerville.

2. The Americans Seize Ticonderoga

THE AMERICAN REVOLUTION did not begin along the vital north-south waterway, but in Massachusetts. For some years Boston had been a focal point of colonial resentment about British policies; as early as 1768, British regular army troops were stationed there to keep the colonists in line. These troops, like all the other British forces in North America, were under the command of Lieutenant General Thomas Gage, who in 1774 was made the governor of Massachusetts as well. The presence of troops did not deter the people of Boston from expressing their continued displeasure with the British, nor from staging the Boston Tea Party late in 1773. In an attempt to squelch the American revolt by stern measures against the Bostonians, the British Parliament passed a succession of acts that not only closed the port of Boston but in effect revoked Massachusetts' charter and destroyed what its citizens considered their basic rights as the King's subjects. Angered by these so-called Intolerable Acts, patriots from the various colonies organized the First Continental Congress in the fall of 1774 to discuss their grievances. Meanwhile, in defiance of Governor Gage's orders, the members of the Massachusetts Assembly set up their own Provincial Congress and took

8

steps to fight if necessary. The Massachusetts Committee of Safety was formed to handle military affairs.

The nucleus of an army already existed in the local militia, for all able-bodied men were obligated to own a weapon, know how to use it, and be ready to serve when needed for defense. Service in the militia was customarily for short periods and local emergencies; the amount and nature of required training varied from one colony to another. But the concept of the citizen being responsible for the defense of his home, town, or colony was well established among the Americans. The British, who relied on a professional army, failed to appreciate the significance of the militia system.

That winter and spring of 1774-75 the Massachusetts militia was alerted, reorganized, and regularly drilled. Military supplies were collected. To cope with emergencies, some of the militiamen were formed into companies of Minutemen, pledged to be ready at a minute's notice if necessary.

On the night of April 18, 1775, General Gage sent a selected force of approximately 600 soldiers to Concord, 22 miles from Boston, to seize some of the colonists' military stores. Reaching Lexington soon after sunrise on April 19, the regulars were confronted by a small company of Minutemen. Someone fired. The first shot was followed by others; when the smoke cleared, eight Americans lay dead and ten wounded. The British, with only one man wounded, marched on to Concord.

At Concord the British found few supplies to seize, for the colonists had already moved or hidden most of their stores. While the Redcoats searched, more and more Americans gathered. Tension mounted, and eventually exploded at the North Bridge. In the exchange of fire, several men from both sides fell. The British then began the march back to Boston, but the militia followed and harassed them. Firing from behind fences or walls, the loosely organized colonials gave the regulars a taste of informal frontier warfare that was sobering in implication. As a British seaman wrote of the Americans, "The enthuseastic zeal with which these people have behaved must convince every reasonable man what a difficult and unpleasant task General Gage has before him."

After pulling back to Boston, where they were under the protection of their warships in the harbor, the British took stock. Their mission had failed, their losses had been heavy, and they had aroused rather than intimidated the rebels. Worse than that, the rebellious militiamen had closed in on Boston; General Gage could see their campfires ringing the town from Charlestown to Dorchester. The British in Boston were now under siege—and would remain so for a year. The war had begun. And for the British, it had begun poorly.

That same day, April 19, General Gage wrote to Major General Guy Carleton, Governor and head of the British forces in Canada, urging him immediately to send reinforcements to Fort Ticonderoga or Fort Crown Point (a smaller post, 12 miles north of Ticonderoga). The north-south waterway must be held. Carleton received the letter too late to act. On May 10, the same day the Second Continental Congress convened in Philadelphia, Fort Ticonderoga was seized by a group of Americans who, according to legend, demanded its surrender "In the name of the Great Jehovah and the Continental Congress!"

Despite the use of its name in this bombastic ultimatum, the Congress knew nothing of the venture. The attack on Ticonderoga was primarily a private affair, although partly instigated by Massachusetts and Connecticut. The Massachusetts patriots had earlier sent a Yale graduate named John Brown to Canada to open discussions with the Canadians. In March 1775, Brown had written from Canada that Ticonderoga should be seized at once if hostilities broke out. He added that the "people on New Hampshire Grants have ingaged to do this Business and in my opinion they are the most proper Persons for this Jobb."

New Hampshire Grants (modern Vermont) had been settled under grants issued by the governor of New Hampshire—a practice that was vehemently contested by New York. Although the British authorities eventually decided in favor of New York, the grantees ignored the decision. The result was a small private war between the New York authorities and the settlers on the Grants, in which the latter were led by Ethan Allen, a large, vehement man of firm conviction, rough manner, and energetic nature.

Allen and his Green Mountain Boys saw the move against Ticonderoga as part of their own vendetta against New York. John Brown, as well as others who were urging Allen to action, were thinking more of the importance of the waterway. To Allen, here was the chance to merge his quarrel with New York into the "general conflict for liberty." As he later wrote, "This enterprise I cheerfully undertook." He was preparing to do just that when Benedict Arnold came on the scene.

Like Allen, Arnold was a strong personality—bold, impetuous, resourceful. He was ambitious and impatient, a stocky, swarthy man of force and action. In his native Connecticut when he heard of the April 19 skirmishes at Lexington and Concord, Arnold summoned the New Haven company of militia, of which he was captain, and threatened to break open the town's magazine if not given powder without delay. Given powder, Arnold and his men hastened to join the gathering American army at Cambridge, just west of Boston. Once there, Arnold soon became restless because of the inactivity. The besieging forces could do little but wait, partly because they had no cannon. What about the British cannon at Ticonderoga? Arnold pleaded with the Massachusetts Committee of Safety to let him seize them. Persuaded, the Committee made Arnold a colonel and empowered him to enlist 400 men to take Ticonderoga and bring back the cannon. Hearing that Ethan Allen was already planning to seize the fort, Arnold left others to recruit his men and rushed ahead to find Allen and demand that he be made commander of Allen's expedition. Allen was not inclined to yield, and the Green Mountain Boys grumbled over the intruder, but Arnold's endorsement by the Massachusetts committee could mean the legal difference between being a "patriot" and an "outlaw." Allen offered Arnold joint command. They led the expedition side by side, each resentful of the other's presence.

At dawn on May 10, the two enterprising leaders and 83 men (all that could cross the lake in the available boats) assaulted the huge, star-shaped fortress of Ticonderoga. A sentry challenged them but his gun misfired; the Americans forced through the gate. Tradition says that Ethan Allen crossed the parade ground to the officers' barracks and yelled up the steps, "Come out, you old rat!" and a half-awake lieutenant, wearing his coat but with his breeches still in his hands, appeared at the top of the steps. The startled officer parleyed until the fort's commander could get dressed; then the surrender was made. There was no bloodshed. The impressive fortress, which required a garrison of thousands to man its positions, had been held by less than 50 soldiers, many of them invalids.

The next day, the attackers moved on and took Crown Point with as little difficulty. In addition, Arnold led a quick raid on Fort St. John's, on the upper Richelieu, where he seized a British sloop, the only British armed vessel on the lake, and assured the Americans temporary control of Lake

Champlain. The outlaw-patriots had quickly gained control of a key segment of the north-south waterway. What appeared more important at the moment, they had acquired a comforting supply of military stores—artillery pieces, lead, and musket cartridges.

The Continental Congress, far from delighted at the news, recoiled in dismay. As no offensive operations had yet been approved, and as the Allen-Arnold expedition was a direct attack on the Crown, the Congress hastened to clear itself of responsibility and ordered Ticonderoga and Crown Point to be abandoned. Furthermore, the captured stores and cannon would be moved to the southern end of Lake George and guarded, with careful inventory being taken to ensure their proper return to the Crown when all the trouble was over. Obviously the Congress was not yet fully convinced that full-fledged war was the only solution to the colonies' difficulties.

Allen and Arnold protested—vigorously—the idea of abandoning the forts. So did New York and New Hampshire, for both those colonies would be vulnerable to British attack from Canada if Ticonderoga were not held. Connecticut offered four militia companies to man the forts. Massachusetts was the most insistent of all; she wanted those cannon to use at Boston. The Continental Congress bowed to pressure: it instructed that the forts would be held. The battle for the great American waterway had begun. For the Americans, it was instinctive, rather than studied, strategy.

The decision to hold Ticonderoga forced the Congress to make its second strategic commitment to the Hudson-St. Lawrence waterway, because it brought up the question of Canada. The Canadians, with little to gain by joining either the British or the colonists, preferred to stay out of their conflict. They had declined an invitation to send delegates to the

Second Continental Congress. But Canada could not stay out of a struggle between Britain and the colonies—if the Americans did not bring the war to Canada, the British would.

In mid-1775 the Americans received word that the British commander, General Guy Carleton, was strengthening his forces in Canada. At Boston also the British were being reinforced, and in June the Congress created the Continental Army to forge the militia units of the various colonies into one united body. A tall, reserved Virginia delegate named George Washington was appointed commander in chief. Washington left at once for Boston, and the Congress then turned its attention to the problem of Canada.

If the Americans could defeat the small British forces in Canada before they were reinforced, there was a good possibility they could persuade the Canadians to join them in the struggle against Britain. Even if the Canadians did not actively join the rebellion, if the British army were driven out of Canada, the Americans could face the British at Boston without fear of an invasion from their rear. After much debate, on June 27 the Congress ordered Major General Philip Schuyler to Ticonderoga to command the Northern Department and the invasion of Canada. It was to be the United States' first military offensive, and it began on an apologetic note. With the aim of promoting the "peace and security" of the colonies, Schuyler was ordered to seize control of Lake Champlain and, if practicable, take St. John's, Montreal, and any other parts of Canada—provided "it will not be disagreeable to the Canadians."

3. The Americans Move North

THE AMERICAN ATTEMPT to conquer Canada in 1775/76 was splendid in conception but disastrous in execution. Motivated by military necessity as well as the idealistic goal of "liberating" the Canadians, a pitifully small and miserably equipped American army conducted a two-pronged invasion with the goal of capturing Quebec—the capital and British stronghold. One force, directed by Major General Philip Schuyler, was to take the Lake Champlain—Richelieu River —St. Lawrence River route; a second force, led by Benedict Arnold, was to advance on Quebec from the wilds of Maine.

Philip Schuyler, gentleman, landowner, and devout patriot, was one of northern New York's leading citizens. From his two impressive homes—one in Albany and another at Saratoga on the banks of the Fish Kill (creek)—he managed his estates and took a leading role in local affairs. His military experience was limited, but there were few others better qualified; Schuyler was one of the first major generals named by the Congress. He took command at Ticonderoga in midsummer 1775. Under him was the capable and well-liked Brigadier General Richard Montgomery, but the two generals could not conquer Canada by themselves. Where were the

15

necessary army and navy? Such forces had to be assembled
and trained—at best a slow process. A few militia units
trickled in from New York, but Schuyler, the aristocratic
New Yorker, was disliked by New Englanders, and few of
them joined him. The Congress eventually supplied Schuyler
with some Continental Army units from Connecticut, Massachusetts, and New Hampshire, but whereas General Washington at Boston had time to train his men in the rudiments
of military practice and discipline, General Schuyler at Ticonderoga had no such time. Speed was essential—not only
to beat the severe Canadian winter but to get to Canada before Britain could send substantial reinforcements to General
Carleton.

The precious summer days slipped by. In August the
roving diplomat and adviser John Brown wrote to Montgomery that Carleton was building a fleet along the Richelieu
River that would soon be able to sweep Lake Champlain.
Brown urged immediate action. George Washington was also
pressing for action. He wrote to Schuyler on August 20, pointing out that the season was late. He also told Schuyler of his
idea for a second invasion through Maine, designed to com-
pel Carleton to divide his force. The two arms of the invasion needed to proceed at the same time, and Schuyler agreed
to cooperate. However, he had troubles that prompted him to
write that "if Job had been a General in my situation, his
memory had not been so famous for patience." A navy had
to be pieced together without proper equipment, the local
Indians needed placating, provincial and personal jealousies
kept Schuyler's troops in an uproar, greed and laziness had to
be overcome, and everything the invasion force needed was
in short supply. Schuyler seemed to lack the vigor and ruthlessness needed to push ahead, but Montgomery, determined
to act, sailed north from Ticonderoga at the end of August

General Philip Schuyler. Oil painting (on wooden panel) by John
Trumbull. Courtesy The New-York Historical Society, New York
City.

with a makeshift fleet and 1,700 men. Schuyler quickly joined him, but soon fell ill with rheumatic gout. Schuyler returned to Ticonderoga to concentrate on sending forward the necessary supplies, while Montgomery assumed actual command of the invasion.

Montgomery may have been deficient in men and equipment, but not in courage or determination. His army may have been, as he said, the "worst stuff imaginable for soldiers," but with it he besieged Fort St. John's, on the upper Richelieu. The fort was well garrisoned and had adequate supplies; Montgomery was short of artillery, gunpowder, and food, and his army was weakened by disease. Try as he did, Schuyler could not supply Montgomery with military necessities; shortages were too great, transport too disorganized. St. John's did not fall until November 2, and by then the northern winter was descending. Had Montgomery's invasion started earlier, or had St. John's fallen sooner, the outcome of the Canadian campaign might have been different.

The immediate effect of the fall of St. John's was that British prestige fell. Unable to rally Canadian support to defend Montreal, General Carleton and his small force of British regulars had no choice but to evacuate Montreal, which opened its gates to the Americans on November 13. Heading for Quebec, Carleton's little fleet was becalmed just a few miles after leaving Montreal. The fleeing British were promptly intercepted by the boisterous Americans and bluffed into surrendering. The ragamuffins had temporarily bested the regulars, although Carleton himself, calm and resolute amid seeming disaster, managed to escape in a rowboat. Two days later Carleton arrived in Quebec, where one of his sergeants, Roger Lamb, noted that "The confidence reposed in his talents, inspired the garrison to make the most determined resistance."

By then such resistance was indeed necessary, for Quebec was threatened not only by Montgomery's force advancing from Montreal but also by the second force of the two-pronged invasion.

Arnold's arrival at Quebec in early November marked the end of one of the most notable marches in military history. With 1,100 men recruited from the Continental Army around Boston, Arnold had left Cambridge on September 11. The mission—to travel up the Kennebec and Dead Rivers, across the mountains on the Maine-Canada border, and down the Chaudière to debouch before Quebec. The purpose—to strike Carleton's forces from the rear, force him to divide his army, and make it more likely that the Americans would take either Montreal or Quebec.

From its beginning in September Arnold's expedition met serious trouble. The Kennebec was a swift-flowing river with many falls or rapids that necessitated manhandling both boats and supplies up cliffs or through dense forest. The boats (river bateaux[3]) weighed about 400 pounds when empty, and since the expedition took supplies for 45 days, an educated guess puts the total weight of boats and supplies at well over 100 tons. Understandably, the men were soon suffering from exhaustion and exposure. Even more serious, the bateaux, having been built hurriedly of unseasoned pine, soon began to leak. Water-soaked food supplies began to spoil. The lateness of the season began to catch up with them, and on September 30 one man noted that his wet clothes froze on him during the night.

As they reached the Dead River, the weather worsened; rain, storms, and snow added to the difficulties of alternating swamps and mountains. As more men became ill from exposure, exhaustion, or poor food, some were sent back to

Fort Western, and a log hospital was built for others. The rest continued, but a deluge of rain from October 19 to 21 flooded the entire area, obliterating landmarks and destroying more of the precious food supply. On October 25 a hungry soldier noted that "we are in An absolute danger of starving."

On the night of October 23, Arnold called his officers to a council of war. Under Washington's orders, the expedition was free to turn back if unforeseen difficulties or severe weather made it hazardous to proceed. Undoubtedly influenced by Arnold, the council decided to push on toward Quebec. The invalids and fainthearted were sent back. Arnold himself forged ahead to contact friendly French Canadians and send food back to his starving army. On his own initiative, Colonel Roger Enos, commanding the rear division, decided to abandon the expedition and take his entire command—one-fourth of Arnold's men and the bulk of the remaining food—back to Cambridge. After a nightmare journey through swamps and ponds from the Dead River to Lake Megantic, the expedition reached the Chaudière River, and by November 1 the men were receiving food sent back by Arnold. On November 10, as General Carleton was trying to rally Canadian support to help defend Montreal against Montgomery, Arnold assembled his motley army at Point Levis on the banks of the St. Lawrence opposite Quebec. He had started out with over 1,100 men; he arrived with about 600. Some had turned back; as many as 50 had died. Arnold had estimated that the march would be 180 miles long and take 20 days; it had been 350 miles long and had taken 45 days. And now he had to take Quebec.

Quebec was a formidable walled town, hugging the cliffs above the St. Lawrence. If Arnold could have gotten there a few days earlier, perhaps its French-Canadian citizenry would have welcomed him. However, by the time he was able to cross the river, British soldiers under Colonel Allan Maclean had reached the town and were ready to defend it. Arnold tried to lure them outside the walls to do battle, but Maclean stayed within the fortress, and Arnold was forced to withdraw and wait until Montgomery could join him. In early December, the two American armies were merged under Montgomery's overall command and the combined force of about 1,000 men laid siege to Quebec.

Guy Carleton had slipped into Quebec in mid-November. Behind the town's sturdy and extensive walls, he was now prepared to conduct a no-nonsense defense. He first warned the disloyal to leave the town, which they did; with about 1,800 men, he proposed to hold his fortress until spring, when the St. Lawrence would thaw and help could be expected from Britain. Guy Carleton was a patient man.

Outside the walls, Montgomery and Arnold could not afford patience. Winter had already begun. What was worse, their army would soon disappear, for the men's enlistments expired at the end of December. They could only attack— and pray for success. Montgomery, admitting that he was "not intoxicated with the favors I have received at [Fortune's] hands," wrote to Schuyler that he thought there was a "fair prospect of success. . . . Nothing shall be wanting on my part."

Montgomery kept his word, but the attack was doomed. To gain surprise, the Americans assaulted Quebec in the midst of a blinding snowstorm, on the night of December 30. They made two feints against the walls of the upper town, but their main attacks were against the lower town, led by Montgomery from the west and Arnold from the east.

Montgomery's men met almost instant disaster. Heavy artillery and musket fire from a fortified house mowed them down in the narrow street. Montgomery was killed in the first moments; leaderless, the survivors withdrew. Arnold's assault fared little better, but it took longer to play itself out. He and his men forced one barricade, but Arnold was wounded in the leg and had to be carried back. Captain Daniel Morgan took command. The attackers met temporary success and took a sizable body of prisoners—more than they could guard—so they decided to wait for either Montgomery or their own rear guard to join them. The rear guard never arrived. They held out until after dawn, when at last a sobbing Daniel Morgan gave up his sword. Captain Henry Dearborn, among the over 400 others who were also taken prisoner, expressed the sentiments of all when he recorded in his new journal for the year 1776: "I begun this year in very disagreeable circumstances."

If circumstances were disagreeable for the prisoners (most of whom, including Morgan and Dearborn, were later exchanged and fought again), they were no less so for the rebels who escaped capture. Arnold refused to abandon Quebec. With pathetic bravado, the remnants of the army— the few men who were willing to reenlist, plus a few reinforcements that trickled in—maintained the siege. It was hardly a siege at all, for the Americans could make no attempt to isolate Quebec from the river, which provided easy access into the city by boat or, during the winter freeze, over the ice. Yet the army stayed, more from reluctance to give up than from realistic hope of success. They were cold; they were hungry; smallpox began to spread among them.

Far away in Philadelphia, the Continental Congress was distressed by the failure of the Canadian campaign and the plight of the army. Reinforcements and supplies were ordered, but the situation improved very little. An unusually severe winter made travel difficult, and the distances were formidable: from Philadelphia to Ticonderoga, 350 miles; from Ticonderoga to Quebec, 330 miles. Furthermore, there was no organized military transport system to cover this long route. Even if there had been, men and supplies were hard to come by. There simply were not enough muskets, lead, powder, blankets, shoes, tents, meat, flour, and men to meet the needs of war. Enough reinforcements reached the army at Quebec to boost its strength to 3,000 by May 1776, but they were inadequately supplied and suffering from disease and disintegrating morale.

In addition to sending reinforcements to the Northern Department, the Congress intensified its efforts to convince the Canadians of the advantages of active cooperation with the Americans by sending a special diplomatic commission to Canada "to promote or form a union." Composed of the veteran diplomat, Benjamin Franklin, so old and ill he did not expect to survive the trip (but he did, by some 14 years); Samuel Chase, who later became a justice of the U.S. Supreme Court; Charles Carroll, a Roman Catholic and one of the richest men in the colonies; and Father John Carroll, a Jesuit priest who later became the first archbishop of Baltimore, the delegation was given powers so broad that Charles Carroll considered them "very burthensome." After an arduous trip, the men reached Montreal on April 29, but they soon realized their journey had been in vain. Their first letter to Congress explained matters only too bluntly: "The general apprehension that we shall be driven out of the Province as soon as the King's troops can arrive, concurs with the frequent breaches of promise the inhabitants have experienced, in determining them to trust our people no further." It all boiled down to hard money—money to buy supplies and food and pay for services—and there was no more hard money. Concluding that it was "improper" to propose a union with Canada "till they see our credit recovered, and a sufficient army arrived to secure the possession of the country," the Commission did what it could and went home.

On May 6, 1776, the expected British warships reached Quebec. The reinforced Carleton at once marched out of the town, and the Americans, sick in body and spirit, began a disastrous retreat.

4. The British Move South

THE BRITISH REGULARS that landed at Quebec in May 1776 marked the beginning of Britain's two-year effort to gain control of the Hudson-St. Lawrence waterway.

Caught unprepared when war began in April 1775, Britain could do little that year. Nevertheless, George III was both determined and confident. He insisted, "When once these rebels have felt a smart blow, they will submit."

The King's opinion was shared by George Germain, Secretary of State for the Colonies. Lord Germain, destined to be the leading British minister in the prosecution of the war, was a military man of precision and efficiency. He saw no "common sense in protracting a war of this sort," and he advocated "exerting the utmost force of this Kingdom to finish the rebellion in one campaign." It seemed natural to exert that force against New England, which was clearly the heart of the rebellion. If New England could be isolated from the remainder of the colonies by land, while its fishing and trading industries were blockaded by sea, the pressure might break rebel resistance. Boston should be evacuated because it was strategically a dead end—no major waterway led to the interior to enable the British to use their navy for support, and the rebels were obviously prepared to fight vigorously in the open countryside. New York, not Boston, was where the British offensive ought to begin. If New York and the Hudson waterline were seized and the rebels driven out of Canada, pressure from both directions would put Britain's forces "on New England's back." This, of course, was exactly what the Americans most feared.

During the winter months of 1775-76, British plans evolved and forces were gathered to implement them. Germain threw himself into the task of finding the ships, the provisions, and the men. Britain faced a shortage of soldiers, for the government had no power of conscription, and the war was not popular enough to lure many to enlist. The shortage of men was met by hiring large numbers of mercenaries from several German states. Somehow ships were found, loaded, and dispatched to America. The British Cabinet was so confident of success it committed the blunder of dividing its strength. A campaign (doomed to failure) was ordered for South Carolina, as well as the major campaign to be conducted by General Carleton from Canada and General Sir William Howe from New York. Howe and Carleton were to seize the Hudson-St. Lawrence route and isolate New England.

General Howe, unenthusiastic about the war yet conscientious in his efforts, had replaced General Gage in October 1775 as commander of the British forces in the American colonies. (Carleton was his counterpart in Canada.) Howe was ordered to evacuate Boston and move to New York to be ready for the spring campaign up the Hudson. Since he could not assemble enough ships to move his entire army at once, he stayed through the winter, for his army was safe enough at Boston, as long as the American besiegers were not strong enough to attack. By early March 1776, however, Washington had the cannon from Ticonderoga and had installed them on Dorchester Heights, overlooking Boston Harbor. Forced to leave Boston, the British forces sailed to Halifax, Nova Scotia, to reorganize and await reinforcements. Anticipating Howe's next move, Washington took his Continental Army to New York.

Howe's campaign against New York did not begin until June, and it dragged on throughout the summer and fall. Howe, ever conscious of the need to conserve his army and unwilling to risk its total destruction, waited for reinforcements, appealed for loyalist support, and alternated his military moves with overtures for peace. Washington, although he sustained defeat after defeat, managed to keep his army intact and retain sufficient strength to pose a constant counterthreat to Howe's moves. It was not until November that Howe finally gained control of New York. The elusive Washington retreated across New Jersey and reached safety beyond the Delaware River in Pennsylvania. Then, in a small but brilliant and psychologically important move, Washington recrossed the Delaware on Christmas night and dealt the British embarrassing defeats at Trenton and Princeton. As 1776 ended, it was obvious that the blows dealt by Howe's army had not been sufficient to force the rebels to submit.

In Canada, meanwhile, Carleton's campaign seemed to go well. Weakened by smallpox, desertions, and shortages of all necessities, the little American army retreated. Lieutenant William Digby, one of Carleton's officers, noted in his journal on June 18 that the British pushed them along after the Americans abandoned St. John's: "Thus was Canada saved with much less trouble than was expected." Carleton halted his advance at the northern end of Lake Champlain, and the Americans fell back to Ticonderoga.

After the Americans fell back from Canada, they came

under the steadying hand of Major General Horatio Gates, who had been sent north by the Congress to infuse some strength into the disentegrating force. Schuyler was still in command as well, and neither general was quite sure how he stood vis-à-vis the other. They reached a workable arrangement, however, and Gates took over at Ticonderoga, where he concentrated on reorganizing the army, Schuyler stayed in Albany and concentrated on supplies and administration.

Horatio Gates was not a glamorous general. Born in England, he had been a major in the British army and had seen action in America during the French and Indian War. He resigned in 1772 and returned to America to become a settler. When war broke out, he offered his services to the

General Horatio Gates. Engraving of a portrait by Gilbert Stuart. From the Myers Collection, Manuscript Division; the New York Public Library, Astor, Lenox and Tilden Foundations. Courtesy the New York Public Library.

patriots. Although his fifteen years as a British officer probably made him the most qualified general in the Continental
Army, unfortunately, what Gates gained in military experience he lost in personal presence. He did not look the part of
either the valiant soldier or the dignified gentleman. He was
nearing fifty, but seemed older, being stooped and stout, with
thinning gray hair and the habit of peering nearsightedly
through spectacles perched on his nose.

Yet Gates was both tough and well-respected. He shared
the hard life of his soldiers and worked diligently to improve
their welfare. Of fairly humble origin himself, he did not
hold himself aloof from his men (as Schuyler did), so he enjoyed some measure of their affection. At times, however,
Gates showed pettiness and a lack of that depth of character
that distinguishes the great from the near-great. Even so, the
general's talents were formidable. He was an efficient ad-
ministrator and disciplinarian, while as a field commander
he tended to be more cautious than bold, more sound than
daring. His military conservatism and personal appearance
led his troops to nickname him "Granny Gates"; the British
general Burgoyne reportedly called Gates the "Midwife."

At Ticonderoga that summer of 1776, Gates faced an
overwhelming problem. His army was a shambles and the
British were poised at St. John's, ready to move south. Gates
realized that his only possible course was to contest control
of Lake Champlain. He ordered Benedict Arnold to build a
navy.

The Americans already had the schooner *Royal Savage*,
two other schooners, and a sloop on Lake Champlain. To
supplement these, Arnold decided to build armed vessels
called row galleys and gondolas. The shipyard would be
Skenesboro, the estate of Philip Skene, a wealthy Tory who
had fled. Located on Wood Creek a few miles upstream from

its outlet near the southern end of the lake, Skenesboro (now Whitehall) had a saw mill and a forge. The call went out to the coastal areas for ship carpenters, riggers, oarmakers, and sailmakers. Promised high wages, they came, bringing their tools with them. Axemen started felling the virgin timber from which the ships were to be built.

Meanwhile, at the northern end of Lake Champlain, a similar scene was being enacted. Carleton had to have ships in order to move his force southward; if the Americans were going to challenge him on the lake, he must also have a fighting navy. Carleton had a fleet of warships on the St. Lawrence, but with their deep draft, they could not navigate a 10-mile stretch of shoal water on the Richelieu River that separated them from Lake Champlain. As determined as Arnold, Carleton ordered the ships knocked apart, hauled overland, and reassembled on the lake. In addition, 10 gunboats had been sent to him disassembled from England, to be assembled on the lake, and 10 more were built at St. John's. Still not content that he had sufficient strength, Carleton brought the ship *Inflexible* up from Quebec. *Inflexible* was 85 feet long and mounted 18 12-pound guns. Alone she could dominate the lake, but after she had been dismantled to reach the lake, it took 28 days to rebuild her. When finally ready to sail in mid-October, the British fleet, in addition to the *Inflexible,* boasted the schooners *Maria* and *Carleton,* one radeau (a large, hard-to-maneuver raft that played little part in the coming battle), one large gondola, 20 gunboats, and a flotilla of longboats and bateaux to transport the army and its supplies.

The American fleet was outnumbered and outgunned. Arnold had nothing to match the *Inflexible*; his total fleet consisted of only 15 vessels—two schooners, one sloop, four row galleys, and eight gondolas.[4] Being at such a disadvantage, he had to devise a strategy that would enable him to make maximum use of the limited forces at his command. His strategy was a simple one. He chose a spot between Valcour Island and the New York (western) shore, about 50 miles north of Ticonderoga, where he could wait, unseen from the main channel of the lake. There he positioned his ships in a crescent-shaped battle line and waited for the British.

Arnold's plan worked. On the morning of October 11 the British fleet sailed by on the eastern side of the island before seeing him. To face him they had to come back against the wind—out of battle order. Since the channel was only three quarters of a mile wide between Valcour Island and the mainland, the British were unable to bring their entire fleet to bear at once.

Captain Georg Pausch, a German artilleryman in the British service, later wrote a vivid description of the fight as it appeared to him. He told how the Americans "had several armed gondolas, which, one after another, emerged from a small bay of the island firing rapidly and effectively. . . . Our attack with about 27 batteaux armed with 24, 12, and 6 pound cannon and a few howitzers became very fierce; and, after getting to close quarters, very animated." The British warships moved up in turn; then one of the American vessels, having been hit several times, began to career to one side, "but in spite of this continued her fire. The cannon of the Rebels were well served."[5]

The battle began about 10:30 A.M., according to Captain Pausch, who also noted that "Close to one o'clock in the afternoon, this naval battle began to get very serious." Both sides fought with determination, but even though the American losses were more serious than those of the British, there was no let-up in the battle. The pounding went on throughout the afternoon; that night the British formed a chain of bateaux to prevent the rebels from escaping to the south.

Benedict Arnold may have been beaten, but he was not finished. As the fog rolled in, he ordered the remainder of his crippled fleet to slip through the British guard, close to shore. Not a ship could still be sailed; so the men rowed—all night and all the next day. The British pursued and sank several of the American vessels, but Arnold got in a final moral blow by grounding and burning his flagship rather than striking her colors. Many of the men escaped through the woods to Ticonderoga, but Arnold's fleet was decimated. The Americans lost 10 of their 15 vessels, and over 80 men killed or wounded.

Despite his defeat and heavy loss in the battle of Valcour Island, Arnold emerged the long-term victor, because disputing control of Lake Champlain and forcing Carleton to build a fleet delayed Carleton's planned invasion until the fall. Although the British now had control of the lake, the severe northern winter was about to begin. Knowing his army could not survive without shelter, Carleton, rather than pressing his advantage, withdrew into Canada to take up winter quarters. Not until spring could Carleton renew his campaign; the battle at Valcour had bought the colonists a year of time, and time worked on their side. The Americans needed time to unite and mobilize, and the same period of time tended to make the British wearier of the struggle and the French more willing to intercede on the Americans' behalf.

Although in retrospect the little naval battle at Valcour Island ranks as an important contribution to American victory in the Revolution, in the fall of 1776 the colonists' military situation seemed grim indeed. The invasion of Canada had been a miserable failure; New York was lost; the Continental Army was constantly suffering from shortages of men and supplies. Yet there must not be despair; the colonists knew they faced hard fighting in 1777, for on July 4, 1776, in defiance of failure and in absolute commitment to success, the Congress had issued the Declaration of Independence. Until that time the patriots had been intent upon winning their rights as subjects of the King; thereafter, they were determined to obtain their complete independence from Britain. Now there could be no reconciliation, no going back.

In London, Lord Germain, disappointed that the 1776 campaign had not brought about the desired collapse of the rebellion, busied himself outlining British strategy for 1777. At first General Howe, writing from America, proposed two offensives for his army—one up the Hudson and one into New England. This coincided with the original British strategy for a concentrated effort against New England, but later Howe decided that the rebellion was on the verge of collapse and the most advantageous move would be to seize Philadelphia, the rebel capital. This he proposed to do with the bulk of his army, suggesting that the other offensives could wait. Germain received this letter of Howe's on February 23; on March 9 Germain wrote Howe that his reasons for striking south were "solid and decisive," and his plan was approved.

While Howe and Germain were exchanging letters to agree on Howe's actions for 1777, Germain was also planning the Canadian campaign for the next summer. Whereas communication with Howe was slow and difficult, the plans for Canada were not so handicapped. Germain had decided that Carleton should not lead the northern advance in 1777, and the man eventually chosen to replace him—John Burgoyne—was readily available in London.

John Burgoyne, then in his mid-fifties, had already achieved considerable success in a varied and turbulent career. Born to modest means and plagued by an unproven scandal over the legitimacy of his birth, he nevertheless married well and worked his way steadily, even aggressively, upward in society, politics, and the army. Like many men who seem driven by some inner force, Burgoyne was of complex

General John Burgoyne. Engraving by Alexander Ritchie. From the Emmet Collection, Manuscript Division; the New York Public Library, Astor, Lenox and Tilden Foundations. Courtesy the New York Public Library.

character. As a writer, he was talented enough to create plays that were sharply drawn and well received. As a member of Parliament, he was an active and conscientious politician. As a military man, he made a reputation during the Seven Years' War as a cavalryman who favored boldness, swift movement, and surprise. Dashing and debonair, he was confident to the point of egotism, ambitious and aggressive to the point of

ruthlessness. His nicknames tell much about his image—
"Gentleman Johnny," "General Swagger," or "Julius Caesar
Burgonius."

Yet as an officer, Burgoyne was far ahead of most of his
contemporaries, for he was sensitive to the roles of individual
and mass psychology. At a time when harsh discipline was
relied on to keep the soldier in line, Burgoyne insisted that
soldiers should be well treated. He looked upon them as fellow human beings, and they responded with affection and
loyalty, even when reverses mounted.

As a major general, Burgoyne served under Gage in
Boston from May to December of 1775. There seemed to be
no future for him there, and he returned to England to urge
the Ministry to launch the Canadian campaign in 1776. During that campaign he served under Carleton, and at the end
of 1776 he again sailed for London, bitter that the campaign
had ended with the loss of the "fruits of our summer's labor
and autumn victory." With characteristic assertiveness, Burgoyne then set about obtaining the Canadian command for
himself. Capitalizing upon Carleton's failure in 1776 as well
as personal friction that had developed between Carleton and
Germain, Burgoyne not only made himself constantly acces-
sible, but on February 28 wrote for the Ministry a lengthy
paper entitled "Thoughts for Conducting the War from the
Side of Canada."

The basic plan of action outlined in Burgoyne's
"Thoughts" became the British plan for the Canadian campaign of 1777. A major force would move south from Montreal to Albany on the upper Hudson, while a diversionary
force moved east from Lake Ontario, down the Mohawk
valley to join the main force on the Hudson. It was anticipated
that at Albany the northern army would join General Howe's
army pressing north from New York. Junction with Howe

was the immediate objective of the campaign, yet when the plans for Canada were drawn, Germain had already approved Howe's plan to move against Philadelphia. The British strategy for 1777, although seeming to be the same as for 1776, had lost cohesion and become vague. What was the long-term objective—to isolate New England? If so, why wasn't Howe instructed to act in conjunction with Burgoyne? And if the strategy was not aimed at seizing the line of the Hudson, what was the purpose of Burgoyne's advance to Albany? One explanation of the muddle is that the Ministry was supremely confident that Howe could complete his Philadelphia campaign in time to move up the Hudson to join Burgoyne in the fall of 1777. It is possible that Germain and the Ministry, misled by the optimism of their generals and their own belief that the rebels were weak, the loyalists were strong, and the rebellion was on shaky ground, did not see the need for concentrated effort against one goal at a time, or at least close coordination of efforts.

With high hopes that his aggressiveness was just what was needed for success, John Burgoyne was promoted to lieutenant general and given command of the expedition from Canada. Carleton would remain as governor, while giving up his military command. Carrying with him orders to "force his way to Albany," Burgoyne sailed for Canada.

The buoyant Burgoyne reached Quebec on May 6, 1777, and made his way to Montreal to confer with the man he was replacing. If he had feared any unpleasantness from Carleton, the meeting quickly set his mind at ease. Despite the humiliation of having his command taken away from him, Carleton was too much a gentleman to be petty. During the succeeding weeks, Carleton cooperated with Burgoyne to the fullest possible extent, but unfortunately the governor was unable to provide all the additional support the army needed.

Burgoyne and Germain had counted on recruiting Canadians, American loyalists, and Indians to supplement the regular troops, but although some such troops were raised, they were fewer than desired. The Canadians just wanted to be left alone; the number of loyalists willing to fight had been greatly overestimated; and not enough Indians responded to promises of plunder. Neither was Carleton able to help Burgoyne obtain all the horses and wagons that would be needed for the campaign; the Canadians were reluctant to sell or lease them to the British army. To make up for the shortage of wagons, 500 light, two-wheeled carts were ordered built. Meanwhile the countryside was to be scoured for horses, needed not only to pull the carts but to draw the expedition's artillery pieces.

While preparing his expedition to move, Burgoyne had a chance to digest a message from General Howe, written April 2 and making clear that Howe intended to head for Philadelphia and that the Northern Army's advance would have "little assistance" from him. If Burgoyne was perturbed, it did not show. Perhaps he was sure that Howe would soon receive definite orders to move up the Hudson; perhaps Burgoyne himself had not tried to fit his campaign into a wider strategy.

Early in June, Burgoyne began collecting his army from its winter quarters and moving up the Richelieu to St. John's. It was a good army, if in some ways a strange one. The bulk of it consisted of approximately 3,700 British infantrymen and 3,000 German infantrymen (all mercenaries, most of them from Brunswick). In addition, there were close to 500 British and German artillerymen, who were needed to handle the expedition's formidable arsenal of no less than 138 cannon. The men themselves, British and German alike, were well-trained, experienced soldiers. Many of them had served in the campaign of 1776, and some effort had been made to

adapt their basic European, formal tactics to American conditions. Supplementing the regulars were the auxiliaries—
about 250 Canadians and loyalists, while the Indians, who
came and went and hence were hard to count, were perhaps
400. The expedition totaled some 7,800 men. Accompanying
them, as was customary in the 18th century, were as many as
1,000 noncombatants—musicians for the regimental bands,
cooks and sutlers, and women camp followers. Many of the
camp followers were wives of soldiers and served the army as
laundresses; several of the officers also had their wives with
them.

The army was well officered. Burgoyne himself enjoyed
the confidence and respect of both officers and men—an extremely important factor in any campaign. In the words of
Lieutenant Anburey, who had served in the campaign of
1776, Burgoyne "joins to the dignity of office, and strict attention to military discipline, that consideration, humanity,
and mildness of manners, which must ever endear him to all
who have the happiness to be under his command."

The army was divided into two divisions, British and
German, and each in turn was organized into brigades composed of several regiments. Officers even down to the regimental level were capable men, but their overall commanders
were outstanding. Burgoyne's second-in-command was Major
General William Phillips, an unorthodox, vigorous gunner.
Brigadier General Simon Fraser led the British Advanced
Corps, an elite force consisting of the grenadier and light infantry companies from each regiment.[6] The steady and re-
liable Major General Friedrich von Riedesel commanded the
Germans. He was soon to have his lovely wife and three small
daughters with him, and Baroness von Riedesel's journal is
one of the most interesting of the contemporary accounts of
the campaign.

Despite its strengths—well-trained men, capable officers, and a strong artillery train—the army had weaknesses. The German mercenaries were essential—the army could not attempt the campaign without them—yet even though they were respected as dependable and brave soldiers, they could not be expected to fight with the same ardor as if they had a personal stake in victory. Few of them spoke English (even Burgoyne and von Riedesel had to converse in French), and small frictions arose between British and German units, with each tending to blame the other for any shortcoming. More serious, the Germans' military organization, attention to disciplined formations, and cumbersome equipment made them a relatively slow-moving force—hardly the most suitable military approach for a wilderness campaign.

Still more serious, the army, even before it left St. John's, was having supply problems. Replacement uniforms for the British regulars had not arrived, and the traditional long tails of their red coats were cut off to use as patches, while their brimmed hats were trimmed to skullcaps. As this change actually made the uniform more practical for the wilderness, the lack of replacements was unimportant, but it foretold other shortages that would be significant in the weeks ahead. There were supply problems in their local transportation, also. Not nearly enough horses had been found, and as Lieutenant Anburey observed, "Another great disadvantage . . . is, that we have to transport all our provisions with us." Indeed they did, and the farther they advanced, the farther those supplies would have to be carried—when possible by boat, elsewhere by cart or wagon. Already many of the quickly built carts had broken down on the road to St. John's.

The optimistic Burgoyne was not one to dwell on difficulties, and as the army assembled at St. John's the atmosphere was positive. Their lake fleet was waiting—the familiar *Inflexible, Maria,* and *Carleton,* as well as smaller vessels—and the army was soon embarked. It was an impressive sight—an entire army, resplendent in uniforms of scarlet and green and blue and white, moving across a beautiful lake in untouched wilderness, en route to capture a fort, and ultimately to seize a continent. Lieutenant Anburey thought it was "one of the most pleasing spectacles I ever beheld." The weather was fine and clear, he noted, and the army formed

the most compleat and splendid regatta you can possibly conceive. . . . In the front the Indians went with their birch canoes, containing twenty or thirty in each; then the advanced corps in a regular line, with the gunboats, then followed the *Royal George* and *Inflexible,* . . . with the other brigs and sloops following; after them the first brigade in a regular line, then the Generals Burgoyne, Phillips, and Riedesel in their pinnaces; next to them were the second brigade, followed by the German brigade, and the rear was brought up with the sutlers and followers of the army. Upon the appearance of so formidable a fleet, you may imagine they were not a little dismayed at Ticonderoga, for they were apprised of our advance, as we every day could see their watch-boats.

On June 21 the fleet put in at the mouth of the Bouquet River, on the lake's western shore, where the army camped for the night. The army's Indian contingent had gathered to meet Burgoyne, and he went ashore to address them. The Indians were of dubious value as soldiers, for they were notoriously unreliable for steady fighting, as well as almost impossible to discipline. They were looked upon with mingled fear, disgust, and amusement; their barbarous methods of fighting were shocking, even to seasoned soldiers. Yet the Indians were valuable for scouting and reconnaissance, for they knew the wilderness and could function in it as no white man could. Burgoyne saw his Indian auxiliaries in another light as well—as a psychological force to invoke fear. He was confident he could control any excesses of cruelty, and when he spoke to them at the Bouquet River encampment he urged them to "regulate your passions when they overbear . . . it is nobler to spare than to revenge, to discriminate degrees of guilt, to suspend the uplifted stroke, to chastise and not to destroy." It was a long and pompous speech, in which Burgoyne positively forbade bloodshed except in combat, and insisted that women, children, and prisoners must on no account be scalped. Scalps could be taken from the dead, but not from the wounded or dying; compensation would be paid for prisoners. Perhaps his speech eased Burgoyne's conscience, but it is hard to believe he expected the painted savages to understand or obey.

Whatever Burgoyne expected, he clearly intended to use his Indians as a terror weapon. In a proclamation issued to all Americans, he appealed to all inhabitants to side with the King. If they did not, he warned, he had only to "give stretch to the Indian forces under my direction." This proclamation was widely circulated. Americans laughed, but they also checked their muskets and kept a close watch on this self-assured general descending on them from the north.

Burgoyne's army moved slowly down the lake. The Americans made no attempt to hold Crown Point, and by June 30 the British army was encamped there. They way to Ticonderoga was open, and that night Burgoyne addressed his troops. Anburey wrote in his journal the following extract of the general's speech:

> This army embarks to-morrow to approach the enemy. The services required of this particular expedition, are critical and conspicuous. During our progress occasions may occur, in which nor difficulty, nor labor, nor life are to be regarded. This army must not retreat.

It was to be all or nothing.

5. Burgoyne Captures Ticonderoga

ON THE AMERICAN SIDE, when Major General Arthur St. Clair arrived in mid-June 1777 to take command of the fortress of Ticonderoga, he found little to cheer him. Morale was low. The legacy of the miserable campaign of 1776 was heavy in the air. John Hawk wrote to his wife on July 1 that the army's record so far had been "but a series of disgraceful defeats, or more disgraceful retreats. . . . We are now at Ticonderoga, and to-day General Burgoyne . . . has put forth a pompous proclamation, which is probably intended to frighten us into desertion or a surrender."

The atmosphere was further depressed by recurrent friction in the Northern Department command. Generals Gates and Schuyler had had difficulty working together, and their respective authority was not always clear. The Congress tried to resolve the issue in March 1777 when it replaced Schuyler with Gates, only to restore Schuyler to command two months later. As Colonel James Wilkinson noted, "These caprices were unworthy of the national councils, and injurious to the public interests." Since Gates was unwilling to serve under

Schuyler, General St. Clair was appointed to hold Fort Ticonderoga against any British attack.

St. Clair, although young, was a respected military figure. A Scot by birth, he had served in the British army before moving to America, and since 1775 had distinguished himself in the American cause. Tall, with an imposing bearing and a pleasant manner, St. Clair had the personal and professional attributes necessary for military success, but at Ticonderoga there were few other elements of success working in his favor.

Not only were St. Clair's men discouraged, but the fort's defenses were in bad repair. Provisions were in short supply and the garrison was less than 3,000 men fit for action—only a fraction of the force needed, for to stop Burgoyne, St. Clair should man Ticonderoga's outlying positions as well as the huge fort itself. Otherwise the British could surround and isolate the fort and eventually force the surrender of its garrison.

Since Ticonderoga was considered the key to holding the Hudson waterway, why was it so poorly prepared? Constant shortages, a long and difficult supply line, and the lack of accurate intelligence explain much. In the spring of 1777, General Washington had not expected the British to invade from Canada that year. He had deemed it necessary to concentrate the bulk of the Continental Army in the south, ready to counter any move General Howe might make from New York. When it became obvious that the British were once more threatening to sweep down from Canada, the Americans did what they could to reinforce Ticonderoga. Just before Burgoyne appeared, St. Clair received a reinforcement of 900 militiamen, but the limited supply of food and ammunition made a larger reinforcement impractical.

Despite the fort's weaknesses, St. Clair was ordered to

hold Ticonderoga as long as possible. Surveying his prospects, he could envisage success only if Burgoyne limited himself to a frontal assault on the fort itself.

During the first few days of July, Burgoyne moved up his army with caution, not knowing the fort's true strength. Intent on cutting off the garrison's escape routes before assaulting the fort with his artillery, he put his troops ashore on both sides of the lake, some four miles above Ticonderoga.

The Germans landed on the eastern shore, where they were to circle inland and cut the retreat route from Mount Independence, a fortified hill on the lake's eastern shore. The lake being only two-thirds of a mile wide at this point, Mount Independence and Ticonderoga were connected by a floating bridge.

The Germans made slow and painful progress. The terrain was wild, overgrown, and swampy, for which the Germans found their uniforms unsuitable. High brass helmets banged against tree branches, long sabers caught on underbrush, heavy boots stuck in mud.

For the British, who landed on the western shore, the going was a little better. They worked their way around the western approaches to the fort, thereby preventing any possible escape by way of the portage to Lake George.

Meanwhile, Burgoyne was preparing to bring his cannon to bear on Ticonderoga, in anticipation of mounting the frontal assault that St. Clair also expected. About July 3, Burgoyne had a stroke of luck—one of the few that were to come his way. One of his engineers, Lieutenant William Twiss, spotted Mount Defiance (also called Sugar Hill) and correctly assessed that cannon placed on its summit would command both the fort of Ticonderoga and the narrow surrounding waters. It was a very rugged hill (one reason the

Americans had not fortified it), but it could be climbed, and Twiss felt sure he could get artillery pieces to the top. Delighted, Burgoyne told Twiss to erect a battery.

Late in the afternoon of July 5, General St. Clair became aware that the enemy were setting up artillery on Mount Defiance. He was checkmated. There was no time to dwell on American blunders or unpreparedness. Feeling that it was folly to wait until Burgoyne completed the battery on Mount Defiance, as well as the encirclement operation underway, he called a conference of his senior officers. They were unanimous for evacuation. The move began immediately after dark. By the early morning hours of July 6, the Americans had crossed the bridge from Ticonderoga to Mount Independence. The wounded and sick, some artillery and stores, and about 500 soldiers led by Colonel Pierce Long started for Skenesboro in the available boats. St. Clair and the remainder, between 2,400 and 2,600 men, started on foot, taking the only road still open, to Castleton, in the hills of Vermont.

By daybreak Burgoyne and his officers realized that the Americans had managed to escape. General Fraser was no laggard, and he soon had his advance corps moving across the bridge to Mount Independence. Again the British had a stroke of luck. Four American gunners had been left behind to man a battery of cannon and hold the bridge; as Lieutenant Anburey observed, had these men carried out their orders, they would have done "great mischief." But the advancing British found the four rebels asleep—dead drunk beside a cask of Madeira. Pouring unchecked across the bridge, Fraser's troops pressed hard after the retreating rebels. Most of his Indians, who could have given valuable help in scouting, preferred to stay behind and loot Ticonderoga, during which process they got drunk.

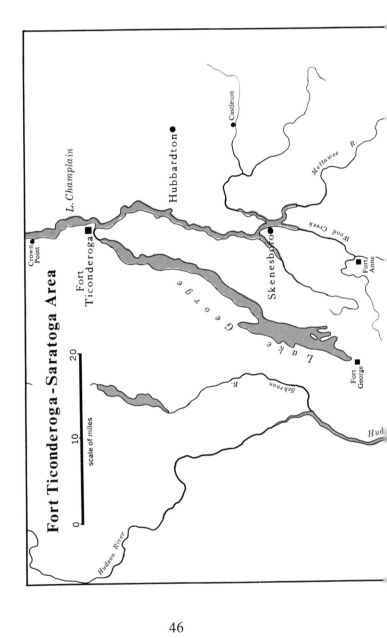

Fort Ticonderoga-Saratoga Area

scale of miles

0   10   20

Crown Point

L. Champlain

Fort Ticonderoga

Hubbardton

Castleton

Mettawee R.

Wood Creek

Skenesboro

Fort Anne

Lake George

Fort George

Schroon R.

Hudson River

Hud

46

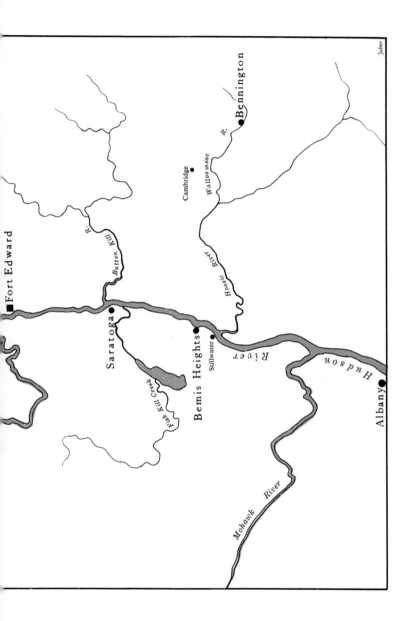

Fort Edward

Bennington

Cambridge

Walloomsac R.

Batten Kill R.

Hoosic River

Saratoga

Bemis Heights

Stillwater

Fish Kill Creek

Hudson River

Albany

Mohawk River

Jaber

47

St. Clair also pressed hard, pushing his small command without mercy. As the sun rose, the day grew oppressively hot; the country through which they moved was a confusion of heavily wooded hills with numerous small ponds and lakes. The road was a mere wagon track, partly overgrown. Nonetheless, the Americans moved rapidly, passing around the northern end of Lake Bomoseen, through the frontier settlement of Hubbardton and on to Castleton.

Not until then did St. Clair call a halt. He had brought the bulk of his command 30 miles from Mount Independence. They were now only 14 miles from Skenesboro, where he hoped to join those who had evacuated by water the next day.

Unfortunately, not all units had been able to keep up the killing pace of St. Clair's march. The rear guard, three regiments of Continentals—a Vermont regiment under Colonel Seth Warner, a Massachusetts regiment under Colonel Ebenezer Francis, and a New Hampshire regiment under Colonel Nathan Hale (not the Nathan Hale who was hanged as a spy but regretted he had only one life to give for his country)—lagged behind. Exhausted from the heat and the march, the rear guard, probably about 1,000 strong, settled down for the night at Hubbardton.

Not far behind them, Fraser and his men also halted for the night. Knowing that the American rear guard was not far ahead, Fraser and Von Riedesel, whose command was behind Fraser's, agreed that if Fraser met up with the Americans and found them too strong for him, he would wait for Von Riedesel to bring up the German troops.

Fraser and his force of 750 men were underway as planned by 3:00 A.M. Within two hours they came upon Hale's regiment cooking breakfast. In the wild confusion the rebels broke for the woods. The British soldiers moved on to confront Warner's and Francis's regiments. Warned by the

opening shots, the two colonels were able to organize themselves enough to deliver an initial volley that slowed down the
leading British platoon. Thereafter, the fighting was intense,
bitter, and disorganized. After their opening volley, the
Americans scattered, taking every advantage of the terrain.
The country was heavily wooded; in the partially cleared
fields, felled trees still lay on the ground, posing obstacles to
orderly movement, yet offering cover to fight behind. The
Americans held a slight edge because they were more accustomed to fighting under such conditions. Less well trained
and less severely disciplined than the British, they tended to
break apart and fight more as individuals, copying the Indian
tactics of hiding behind cover and aiming their fire at individual targets. The British, on the other hand, were trained to
act in close-order formation, standing shoulder to shoulder
to close ranks and firing volleys on command. The effective-
ness of such volleys was based on simultaneously firing
enough shots to create the proverbial hail of bullets. Volley
fire was not aimed, for Brown Bess muskets did not have
sights for aiming.

At Hubbardton, the left side, or flank, of Warner's front
was against a steep and rugged hill. Fraser sent a picked force
to climb the hill, outflank the rebels, and cut the retreat road
to Castleton. Fraser's men executed the maneuver, but Warner's men merely pulled their lines back and kept fighting.

Fraser's situation became critical. His troops had suffered many casualties, including three officers wounded, and
the Americans threatened to seize control of the battle. Fraser
sent word to Von Riedesel to hurry. Meanwhile, almost in
desperation, he ordered a bayonet charge. At that moment,
the welcome noise of German psalm-singing announced that
Von Riedesel's troops were arriving. Dripping with sweat and
cursing the slowness of his men, Von Riedesel threw his lead-

ing corps into the fight, keeping up the blare of bugle, drum, and voice to give the impression of a larger force. Despite their haste, the Germans were still in good order. Their disciplined volleys quickly decided the issue. Colonel Francis was killed, and his regiment faded into the woods. Warner ordered his men to scatter and meet him later in Manchester, roughly 60 miles to the south. Hale and many of his men were taken prisoner.

Uncertain what the rebels would do next, Fraser neither gave chase through the woods nor continued along the road to Castleton. St. Clair's rear guard was scattered, but his main force was still intact.

For the British, the victory at Hubbardton was a costly one. Although American casualties were higher, Fraser's forces sustained nearly 200 casualties, including 35 dead; it had been a grim and hard-fought battle. For what it was worth, the British did have possession of the Hubbardton battlefield. A young lieutenant named William Digby later wrote that "Our men got more plunder than they could carry." Then, with a wry sense of humor, he noted that they could have taken great quantities of paper money, "which was not in the least regarded then, tho had we kept it, it would have been of service, as affairs turned out." Digby, along with many of his comrades, was later to spend time as an American prisoner.

Journeying southward on July 6, Colonel Long, commanding the waterborne part of the American retreat from Ticonderoga, neglected to set up any delaying obstacles along his retreat route. He was confident that the floating bridge, anchored by sunken piers and protected by a large wooden boom, would delay the enemy. However, it took Burgoyne's gunboats less than half an hour to ram through the bridge and boom and start to chase the unsuspecting Americans. Overtaking Long's party at Skenesboro, Burgoyne captured or destroyed nearly all the American fleet, together with cannon and provisions. Nevertheless, the bulk of the rebel force managed to escape to Fort Anne, a small post on upper Wood Creek some 15 miles south of Skenesboro.

Taking possession of Skenesboro, Burgoyne ordered Lieutenant Colonel John Hill to pursue the rebels. Hill, with less than 200 men, set out in pursuit, arriving close to Fort Anne by nightfall. Hill was tricked into believing that the Americans were at Fort Anne in strength, so he decided not to attack at once. Early the next morning, July 8, his small group was attacked by an invigorated American force. A new factor—the local militia—had begun to affect events. Long had just been reinforced by Colonel Henry Van Rensselaer and about 400 New York militia. The Americans soon had Hill and his men surrounded and fighting for their lives. It might have ended badly for Hill had not the Americans run low on ammunition. The rebel force retreated, leaving Hill's men shaken but intact. Badly disorganized and unable to make a stand, the Americans burned Fort Anne and then fell back 15 to 20 miles to Fort Edward on the upper Hudson River. Meanwhile, St. Clair and his forces from Ticonderoga, their retreat cut off, began a circuitous route through the hills from Castleton to reach Fort Edward by July 12.

Almost exactly a year earlier, the Congress had issued the Declaration of Independence, committing the colonists to a fight for their freedom from Britain. Now, during the first two weeks of July 1777, rebel fortunes seemed to have reached a new low. Ticonderoga, widely believed to be the key to defense from the north, had fallen with ridiculous ease, and only a small and demoralized army stood between Burgoyne and Albany.

6. A Crucial Delay

GENERAL BURGOYNE, after the heady successes of the previous few days, concentrated his army at Skenesboro, which only a year before had served as an American shipyard. Making himself comfortable as the houseguest of the loyalist Philip Skene, Burgoyne considered his next move. He had been underway only a month, and he was now within 70 miles of Albany. No obstacles to compare with Ticonderoga stood in his way, and the rebels were in full retreat—almost panic.

As a professional soldier, Burgoyne understood the fundamental military principle that a defeated and demoralized enemy should be pursued aggressively until a definitive victory is obtained. Yet at this important time, Burgoyne did not send his most mobile forces in rapid pursuit, but instead chose to advance at a much slower pace with his entire army, including much of the cumbersome artillery train. The pace was slowed still further by Burgoyne's choice of route to the Hudson. From Skenesboro, there were two possible routes. One involved backtracking to Ticonderoga, making the short portage to Lake George, and then traveling by water to Fort George, at the lake's southern tip. From there a good road led to Fort Edward, only about 12 miles away.

The second route, largely overland, led directly south along Wood Creek to Fort Edward. For about four miles the force could travel by water on Wood Creek, using bateaux and small craft, but only a rough wagon track ran through the remaining 15-20 miles of wilderness. In outlining his campaign, Burgoyne had earlier labeled the Lake George route as the "most expeditious and commodious," while the Wood Creek route was "much less desirable."

In effect, Burgoyne's decisions to take the Wood Creek route and to advance with his entire army rather than a fast-moving force delayed his advance almost a month—a time lapse that was to work in favor of the Americans. Why did the general act as he did? Why all the artillery? Why the Wood Creek route?

The proportion of artillery pieces to infantry in Burgoyne's army was much higher than customary in those days, especially for a wilderness campaign. About 400 horses were needed just to pull the cannon, and the horses had to have forage to keep alive. The bulk and weight of the guns and their heavy carriages demanded better roads than men alone required, and by nature they slowed down a march. Nevertheless, Burgoyne considered the cannon essential. Conscious of their psychological effect on undisciplined soldiers, he considered artillery to be "extremely formidable to raw troops." When loaded with grape or cannister shot, artillery was effective in open combat. Another reason, that seems to have carried more weight with him, was his great respect for the Americans' ability to construct formidable field fortifications from earth and logs. Should the Americans choose to build such obstacles in his path, the artillery would be useful.

As for his choice of route, Burgoyne reasoned that to take the Lake George route would have meant a retreat from Skenesboro to Ticonderoga, which would have damaged his army's morale. This may have been an ungrounded fear; as Lieutenant Digby noted in his journal, "Many here were of opinion the general had not the least business in bringing the army to Skenesborough," while the victories of Fort Anne and Hubbardton served "no visible advantages . . . except prooving the goodness of our troops at the expense of some brave men." Digby (and some others) felt Burgoyne should have returned to Ticonderoga and pushed directly down Lake George to Fort George, where there was a chance of capturing a goodly supply of stores, wagons, and horses. Burgoyne apparently hesitated to attack Fort George directly, and argued that the advance from Skenesboro to Fort Edward would force the rebels to abandon Fort George for fear of encirclement. This indeed was what happened—the Americans withdrew from Fort George shortly after Ticonderoga fell, and the British were able to take over the post without a major battle.

One other factor may have influenced Burgoyne's decision in favor of the Wood Creek route. His loyalist adviser and host, Philip Skene, owned the lands along Wood Creek, and if the army went that way, they would have to make great improvements in the wagon track. A good road would improve the value of his lands, and Skene would not have been human had he not hoped this would come to pass. Exactly how much he swayed Burgoyne is uncertain.

The Wood Creek route proved disastrous for Burgoyne, partly because General Schuyler, with a keen appreciation of the desperate consequences of the Burgoyne advance, refused to panic or despair. He realized that at present his entire army—small, disorganized, broken in morale, poorly armed, and short of ammunition—could not possibly fight Burgoyne. They could, on the other hand, obstruct, delay, and harass him. With quiet determination, Philip Schuyler, the aristocrat, began his own version of guerrilla warfare. He sent out small parties to warn the scattered inhabitants that giving aid to the enemy was treason, and that they should drive off their cattle, burn their crops, and destroy or hide their stores of food. Other parties began to sabotage the route from Skenesboro south to Fort Edward. They dug trenches to let the water of the swamps flood the dry land; they rolled huge boulders into Wood Creek to dam its course and send its waters flooding the countryside; they destroyed bridges. Most important, axemen felled trees across the road and stream. This was extremely effective, for the enormous trees of the virgin forest, felled so that their branches interlocked, made formidable barriers that would take hours to chop away. As militia from the surrounding country gradually joined him, Schuyler put more and more of them to work with axes.

Burgoyne made little effort to prevent Schuyler's sabotage. He seemed to feel no need for haste, and he wanted time to let supplies accumulate. He himself remained at Skenesboro, while part of the army set about clearing the road to Fort Edward.

It was nasty work. Clouds of gnats, mosquitoes, and biting flies drove the men wild. The weather was hot and muggy, which affected the Germans in particular; one wrote home that the heat was "uncommonly great." Forty bridges had to be built, and a causeway nearly two miles long had to be laid through a swamp. The trees were almost the last straw. According to Anburey, "You would think it almost impossible, but every ten or twelve yards great trees are laid across the road." Schuyler's guerrilla fighters had done their work well.

At last the road was serviceable. The army left Skenes-

boro, and by July 29 most of the British force had reached
Fort Edward. It was over three weeks since Fort Ticonderoga
had fallen into British hands; the invasion that had begun
with such speed had slowed to a pace of roughly one mile
per day.

On July 27, as the British moved up to Fort Edward, a
young American girl in the area, Jane McCrea, was killed
and scalped by one of Burgoyne's Indians. The details of the
incident will probably never be accurately known, for from
the beginning the episode was charged with emotion. Jane
and an older woman who was seized with her but not harmed,
were loyalist sympathizers who had awaited the British arrival with confidence. The older woman was a cousin of General Fraser's; Jane McCrea was reportedly engaged to a
young man in Burgoyne's army. The scalping was completely
contrary to Burgoyne's "rules of war" as explained to his
Indian warriors. Burgoyne held an inquiry, ordered the Indians to turn over the murderer, and planned to execute him.
At that point, St. Luc La Corne, the Indian leader, insisted
that if Burgoyne did so, the Indians would desert in a body
and go home.

Burgoyne had a problem, hinging on the fine line of dis-
tinction between the organized and ritualized killing of war,
which carries moral sanction, and the act of murder, which
does not. Burgoyne's Indians had promised obedience to his
rules, but violations had occurred. The Jane McCrea incident was not the first. It was, however, destined to be the
most important. Yielding to pressure, Burgoyne pardoned
the killer. Most of his Indians stayed for the time being, but
news of the affair began to spread over the countryside. Many
who had not yet taken up arms to stop Burgoyne began to
reconsider. Even loyalists began to wonder; what did it profit

one to declare for the King, if the King's army offered no better protection than that?

Burgoyne was soon warned of the reaction he might expect. Lieutenant Digby wrote that soon after "the melancholy catastrophe of the unfortunate Miss McCrea," a letter to Burgoyne was found nailed to a tree. It cautioned him not to be too elated over his rapid progress, and ended by suggesting he beware of crossing the Hudson, hinting, "Thus far shalt thou go and no farther."

Schuyler's troops made no attempt to hold Fort Edward, but fell back in prudent retreat. The army, badly disorganized, was still small, although St. Clair and the survivors from Ticonderoga had joined, as well as Brigadier General John Nixon and some 600 reinforcements from Washington's Continental Army. Washington was loathe to send many troops to the north because General Howe had not yet begun his summer campaign, and Washington felt it necessary to hold his army intact to counter any move Howe might make. Nevertheless, in addition to Nixon's brigade, Washington sent Schuyler two major generals—Benjamin Lincoln and Benedict Arnold. The commander in chief hoped that Lincoln, from Massachusetts, could induce more of the New England militia to join the Northern Army. Most of the militia with Schuyler were from New York, for the old New York-New England quarrel still hampered cooperation, and Schuyler, a New Yorker, was disliked and distrusted by New Englanders. So while Lincoln was to bring sectional balance and exert tact to heal internal difficulties, Arnold, the most dashing of the American generals, was to instill confidence and fighting spirit. This was something Schuyler could not do. Poor health prevented his taking an active role in the field, and he was not that sort of man anyway.

Despite the efforts to bolster it, the Northern Army was in grim shape. Retreat demoralizes even the most professional of soldiers, and the pitiful force gradually withdrawing southward was variously described by observers as "in want of all necessaries and even of courage," and a "starved, lousey, thievish, pockey army." It may have been pitiful, but it was all that stood between Burgoyne and Albany. On August 3, Schuyler halted it at Stillwater, on the Hudson River 24 miles south of Burgoyne's force at Fort Edward. Schuyler was determined to retreat no farther.

A month had passed since the fall of Ticonderoga. Burgoyne's army was poised at Fort Edward, with only a weak and demoralized rebel army standing between them and Albany, about 50 miles away. The diversionary attack down the Mohawk valley was already underway and should soon be linking up with Burgoyne's force. Surely now was the time for Burgoyne to thrust forward with all possible vigor.

Yet Burgoyne's army waited. And waited. It waited until mid-September. The problem was as simple as the solution was complex: lack of sufficient supplies.

Burgoyne's supply system was breaking down. Already, while still at Skenesboro, Burgoyne had begun to complain that "I have had to contend against wet weather that rendered the roads almost impracticable at the carrying places. . . . Indeed, the combination of land and water movement, bad roads, inactivity, and sometimes disobedience in the country, and a thousand other difficulties and accidents unknown in other services, disconcert all arrangements."[7] As Lieutenant Anburey put it, "Certainly the situation of the General is extremely trying. . . . For one hour that he can devote in contemplating how to fight his army, he must allot twenty to contrive how to feed it."

The farther the army advanced southward, the worse the situation became, for almost all supplies still had to be sent down the line of advance from Quebec. There simply were not enough horses, bateaux, lake craft, carts, and wagons to maintain a sufficient flow of goods needed by an army numbering close to 9,000, including auxiliaries and non-combatants. Many of the two-wheeled carts broke down, and breakdowns caused bottlenecks at the portages; the remaining carts and wagons were insufficient and overloaded. Burgoyne issued orders that no officer was to use the carts for his personal gear, yet there is evidence that no less than 30 carts were used to carry Burgoyne's own trunks of uniforms, wines, and other accessories to ease the discomforts of the wilderness.

While assembling his forces at Fort Edward in early August, Burgoyne realized that it would be necessary to accumulate sufficient food, ammunition, and hospital stores to build a strong supply base before taking further strides into enemy territory. When he started the next drive, to Albany, his rear communications would be broken, and the army must have sufficient supplies to sustain it until Albany was secured. There seemed no alternative to a halt for accumulating supplies.

During this frustrating delay, General Von Riedesel offered a plan. The army had never had enough horses, and Von Riedesel had learned that there were horses in the area east of Castleton. There were no concentrations of rebels in the area to offer serious opposition, so Von Riedesel proposed an expedition eastward through Castleton to obtain horses. The German general especially wanted horses for his dragoons, who were designed by equipment and training to be mounted troops, but who were serving as infantrymen because of the shortage of horses.

Urgently needing improved transport to speed his army on its way to Albany, Burgoyne agreed with Von Riedesel's plan but changed it in important particulars. Lieutenant Colonel Friedrich Baum was to lead the expedition, not toward Castleton, where rebel opposition was judged to be unlikely, but toward Manchester, where Colonel Seth Warner's regiment was known to have reassembled after the Hubbardton encounter. With startling complacency, Burgoyne instructed Baum that, while it was "highly probable" that Warner's regiment would retreat before him, "should they, contrary to expectation, be able to collect in great force, and post themselves advantageously, it is left to your discretion to attack them or not, always bearing in mind that your corps is too valuable to let any considerable loss be hazarded on this occasion."

Baum was not only to seize 1,300 horses to mount the dragoons, but as many draft horses as possible for the rest of the army; he was also to seize wagons, carriages, draft oxen, and cattle for slaughter. Burgoyne saw Baum's mission as having two other purposes as well: To divert the rebels from the Mohawk valley, where the British diversionary attack was underway, and also to mislead the rebel leaders into believing that Burgoyne's main force was actually going to swing east into New England rather than push south to Albany.

Baum's force was not an elite force of light infantry, designed to move rapidly, but a motley force of Germans (including the dragoons, whose equipment made them clumsy and slow on foot), Loyalists, Canadians, Indians, and a small element of 50 marksmen from Fraser's corps. Their total was close to 800; their effective fighting, or bayonet, strength was about 650. They dragged two artillery pieces with them.

As they were getting underway on August 11, Burgoyne once more changed their destination—to Bennington. Having just learned of a large stock of rebel supplies, including flour, at Bennington, Burgoyne fell into the trap of letting the expedition's task exceed its capabilities. Yet the possible gain was substantial. Later, defending his decision, Burgoyne indicated he felt the risk justifiable "for so great a purpose as that of a supply sufficient to enable the army to follow at the heels of a broken and disconcerted enemy."

Von Riedesel, upon hearing of the change in plan, was filled with "astonishment and fear." He knew that, at Bennington, Baum could be struck not only by Warner's men at Manchester but also by the main American force at Stillwater. The country was rugged; movement would be slow. Von Riedesel also knew that the loyalist who had informed Burgoyne of the stores in Bennington had also warned that rebel resistance in that area would be severe; the informant had suggested sending a force of 3,000 men.

Nevertheless, Burgoyne was confident of success, possibly because he was unduly influenced by the ease of his advance so far (he had not witnessed the only effective rebel resistance at Hubbardton). After all, a quick move by Fraser's corps would prevent the Americans at Stillwater from interfering with Baum's mission. As to local resistance, Burgoyne was optimistic. The countryside, he continued to believe, was predominantly loyalist.

Thus it was that Colonel Friedrich Baum, the unfortunate victim of optimism, overconfidence, and an insufficient margin for error, marched for Bennington, where John Stark and the New England militia would forge what Thomas Jefferson later called "the first link in the chain of successes which issued in the surrender at Saratoga."

7. The Battle of Bennington

THE AMERICAN FORCE that Baum and his men met at Bennington consisted primarily of a brigade of militia raised by New Hampshire and led by Brigadier General John Stark. Both the brigade and its leader were of unusual nature. New Hampshire, alarmed at Burgoyne's advance, desperately sought a way to halt it. They had no capital with which to raise a regiment, but John Langdon, speaker of the New Hampshire General Court, offered the Committee of Safety his personal fortune with which to raise a brigade. He reasoned that New Hampshire could repay him if the Revolution succeeded, while if it failed, his fortune would mean little. Langdon also proposed that the brigade might "safely be entrusted" to "our friend Stark, who so nobly sustained the honor of our arms at Bunker's hill."

Stark had indeed fought well as a Continental officer at Bunker Hill, and again at Trenton; but although a natural leader with a leader's courge, energy, and ability, Stark was also an independent soul whose piercing eyes and tight lips indicated a streak of stubbornness and an equally strong sense of pride. From the first, he had thrown himself enthusiastically into the patriot cause, but in March 1777, Stark was not promoted when the Congress named some new major generals. Taking the rebuff as a blow to his honor, he promptly resigned his commission and returned to New Hampshire, his farm, and his wife Molly. In July, upon receiving a request to lead New Hampshire's new brigade, Stark replied in astounding fashion. He had no confidence, he said, in the command of the Northern Department, but on the other hand if the new brigade was held accountable only to New Hampshire, not to the Congress or the Continental Army, he would command.

Stark won his point. He was commissioned a brigadier general of militia and authorized to act "separately as it shall appear expedient to you for the protection of the people or the annoyance of the enemy." Stark was almost a free agent, and the people of New Hampshire apparently approved. Within a week, he had enlisted nearly 1,500 officers and men for a term of two months. The New England farmers shouldered their muskets and marched across the Green Mountains to Manchester, Vermont.

At Manchester in early August were Colonel Seth Warner's regiment of Continentals and some militia forces, all under the command of General Lincoln. Lincoln now ordered Stark's brigade and the other militia to join Schuyler's main force at Stillwater, but Stark refused. He was accountable only to New Hampshire and he chose to fight his own way. When warned that he was assuming a fearful responsibility, he replied that he had "often assumed responsibilities for the good of his country, and should do so again." Lincoln hurried back to Stillwater, where he and Schuyler wisely agreed to treat Stark as an ally rather than a disobedient subordinate. For the time being Warner and his Continentals remained at Manchester, but Stark, apparently intending to attack Burgoyne's rear, moved his brigade 12 miles south to Bennington. There, on August 13, his scouts told him that a party of Indians were at Cambridge, about 18 miles away to the northwest. Stark promptly sent a force of 200 men to attack them.

The Indians at Cambridge were part of Baum's expedition, which so far had had little success in obtaining horses. The Indians were out of control, antagonizing the countryside by slaughtering cattle to obtain cowbells. On top of that, when Stark's men appeared, Baum realized that his opposition was more numerous than he had anticipated. Simultaneously Stark realized that the Indians were not an isolated raiding party but part of a sizable force. Stark prepared his brigade to move up, and sent word to Warner to join him; Baum sent a report to Burgoyne.

Unfortunately for Baum, who spoke no English, his message to Burgoyne did not convey the urgency of his need. Although he estimated the rebels' strength to be as much as 1,800 men—more than twice his own—he added that they might be expected to retreat before him. Apparently not even considering retreat, Baum asked for reinforcements to enable him to reach Bennington and carry out his original mission.

On August 14 Baum's forward units skirmished with Stark's, but the German colonel moved closer to Bennington until, about four miles from the village, he could see Stark's main force. Outnumbered, he halted, on what Stark later called "a very advantageous piece of ground." Stark also halted, and there the two sides remained through August 15, while the skies poured rain. In that kind of weather, fighting with muskets was impossible.

Meanwhile, Burgoyne ordered Lieutenant Colonel Heinrich Breymann and the 550-man German advanced corps to march to Baum's assistance. The German reinforcements moved slowly, not merely because their orders conveyed no sense of urgency. They took with them two 6-pounder field pieces, which were difficult to handle; the continuous rain turned the dirt track into a quagmire; advance was laborious. By the night of August 15, Breymann's corps had not yet reached even Cambridge. Warner's regiment, on the other hand, got within six miles of Stark before halting for the night. Warner himself rode on to join Stark. When the rain stopped just before noon the next day, the rebel force moved out to attack Baum's positions.

Baum's defense centered on a hill overlooking the Walloomsac River, but his small force was divided into several scattered positions which could not support each other. Against these positions, Stark sent out three columns. While one made a wide flanking movement to surround Baum from his left and another moved in on Baum's right, Stark and the main column would strike directly down the Bennington road toward the Walloomsac bridge. It was a complicated plan for men whom Stark described as not "trained to the art of war."

The American flanking columns moved out first. Stark waited to hear them open fire before advancing in the center. It seems possible that the Americans capitalized on their lack of clearly identifiable uniforms—and on Baum's expectations of loyalist support—to move in close to the British positions before firing. Later, General Von Riedesel (and there were others who agreed with him) stipulated that Stark's men had passed themselves off as loyalists to gain initial advantage. Anyway, the flanking columns began firing around 3:00 P.M. and quickly accomplished the defeat of the isolated groups.

The battle moved on to the hill itself. According to an American eyewitness (in an account later published in the *Pennsylvania Evening Post*): "Our men easily surmounting their breastworks, . . . the enemy at once deserted their covers and ran: and in about five minutes their whole camp was in the utmost confusion and disorder, all their battalions were broken in pieces, and fled most precipitately. . . ." This description was corroborated by the relatively small number of enemy dead and the large number of prisoners taken. So complete was the American victory that Baum's force was essentially destroyed. Baum himself was mortally wounded.

Stark's men suffered few losses (30 dead and 40 wounded by the end of the day), but at the conclusion of this part of the battle they were badly disorganized. Some were still pursuing the few enemy troops that had escaped; some were guarding the numerous prisoners; others were looting the battlefield, for Stark had promised them the plunder. At this moment Breymann's relief corps arrived.

Not knowing that Baum was already defeated, and despite the fact that his own men had marched far and were worn, Breymann pushed his way down the road from the west, thrusting aside the group of Stark's skirmishers who tried to stop him. The Americans fell back, but about sunset, they received reinforcements: Warner's 350-man regiment, having made an unhurried march to the scene, arrived at a crucial moment. Unlike Stark's men, who were exhausted from the exertion of battle in the heat, Warner's regiment was relatively fresh. They were able to check Breymann's advance, and when the German officer assessed his position, he ordered a retreat. Although the rebels pursued, Breymann, himself wounded, saved the bulk of his force by organizing an orderly retreat under cover of darkness.

Breymann's return proved to be Burgoyne's only compensation for an otherwise disastrous venture.

Although later, when seeking to justify his actions, Burgoyne was to call the Bennington defeat "little more than the miscarriage of a foraging party," he would also admit that it had been fatal to the campaign, in that he thereafter realized the sentiment of the country and that he was dependent on force alone. Bennington had cost him more than 10 percent of that force, and there had been no gain whatever.

Well might the *Pennsylvania Evening Post* gleefully report that "poor General Burgoyne is gone 'STARK MAD.' "

Until the defeat at Bennington, Burgoyne had been optimistic to the point of braggadocio. Now his mood was entirely changed. On August 20 he wrote a lengthy letter to Germain in London, detailing his many problems. His overstrained supply lines were choking him, and little was to be had in the way of provisions from the surrounding countryside. Until this point Burgoyne had believed that the people would flock to his side as he advanced, he now confessed to Germain that "The great bulk of the country is undoubtedly with the Congress in principle and zeal." Moreover, Burgoyne, who had previously worried little about the rebel militia, now wrote that "their measures are executed with a secrecy and dispatch that are not to be equalled. Wherever the king's forces point, militia, to the amount of three or four thousand, assemble in twenty-four hours; they bring with them their subsistance, etc., and the alarm over, they return to their farms. The Hampshire Grants in particular . . . abounds in the most active and rebellious race of the continent, and hangs like a gathering storm upon my left."

Furthermore, Burgoyne had received confirming word from Sir William Howe that he intended to move south on Philadelphia, not up the Hudson to Albany. Although Burgoyne had known Howe's plans, Burgoyne later claimed he had thought, judging from the date of Howe's letter (July 17), that Howe had not yet received orders from London to cooperate with the northern army, but would shortly get them. In his August 20 letter to Germain, Burgoyne complained bitterly about Howe's moves: "No operation, my lord, has yet been undertaken in my favor. . . . When I wrote more confidently, I little foresaw that I was to be left to pursue my way through such a tract of country, and hosts of foes, without any co-operation from New York. . . ."

Assuring Germain that "I yet do not despond," Burgoyne prepared to finish stockpiling provisions for 25 days and then move his army across the Hudson, break his supply lines to Canada, and advance on Albany. Before he could do so, he received word from the Mohawk valley of another serious setback.

8. Defeat in the Mohawk Valley

DURING JULY AND AUGUST, while Burgoyne was slowly moving his force from Fort Ticonderoga to Skenesboro to Fort Edward, the scheduled diversionary attack through the Mohawk valley was underway, commanded by Lieutenant Colonel Barry St. Leger. A cool-headed, experienced officer, St. Leger nevertheless had a grave shortcoming: like many other British officers, he despised the rebels and therefore tended to underestimate them.

The purpose of St. Leger's expedition was to push down the Mohawk valley, subdue the rebels, prevent the local rebel militia from joining the main army opposing Burgoyne, gain control of the countryside for the King, and then link up with Burgoyne on the Hudson. Without loyalist support, his chances for success would not be high. But St. Leger had been assured by the Johnson family, the largest landholders in the Mohawk valley, that most of the settlers there were loyal to the King. Even if the people had not yet taken up arms, they would be much more disposed to cooperate if St. Leger and his troops marched victoriously down the Mohawk valley.

Unfortunately St. Leger's force was a small one, numbering less than 2,000. Of these, some 400 were British and

German regulars (including the 40 artillerymen needed to man the expedition's nine small cannon) and another 400 or so were loyalists. The remaining members of the force was Indians—between 800 and 1,000. St. Leger knew he would be heavily dependent on his Indians; he also knew that, although they could and would fight savagely under certain conditions, they were undependable for steady, disciplined effort. Clearly the expedition's success or failure would be determined to a large extent by factors outside St. Leger's control—the support of the local loyalists and the conduct of his Indian auxiliaries.

The expedition left Montreal on June 23, sailing up the St. Lawrence River and across eastern Lake Ontario to reach Oswego on July 25. St. Leger and his men headed eastward by way of Lake Oneida toward the rebel-held post of Fort Stanwix. Situated on the upper Mohawk River, the fort (near the present-day site of Rome) commanded the gateway to the Mohawk valley. It had been built during the French and Indian War, but, as far as St. Leger knew, it was now in disrepair and manned by only 60 men. He expected little opposition there.

Upon reaching the fort on August 3, St. Leger paraded his force in view of its outer walls, hoping to bring about surrender simply by intimidation. Nothing happened. He then sent the fort commander a pompous proclamation. There was no reply. By this time, St. Leger realized the fort was stronger than he had anticipated, so he withdrew to begin preparing for a siege.

Fort Stanwix could not compare with Fort Ticonderoga as a military bastion; but it was nevertheless a major obstacle to St. Leger. During the spring and summer of 1777, the patriots had been busy repairing and rebuilding its fortifications, so that it was now in fair condition and manned by some

750 Continentals. The fort commander was Colonel Peter Gansevoort, a young Dutchman from Albany. His second-in-command was a fiery-spirited lieutenant colonel named Marinus Willett. The two officers were determined to hold the fort. They had food for six weeks, ammunition in reasonable supply, and moral courage. Furthermore, having watched St. Leger's parade and realized that Indians made up the bulk of his force, they knew that both the garrison and the inhabitants of the valley would suffer a hideous fate if the fort fell. Gansevoort and Willett settled down to a war of nerves.

Help was on the way, though, for despite there being much loyalist sentiment in the area, there were also a goodly number of people who favored the patriot cause. Many of these were ardent, independent-minded frontiersmen, the descendants of those staunch German Lutherans of the Palatinate who, having survived the ravages of Europe's Thirty Years War, had come to America fed up with kings and standing armies. The Palatines' leading citizen, an energetic veteran of the French and Indian Wars named Nicholas Herkimer, was chairman of Tryon County's committee of safety and the commanding general of its militia. As soon as Herkimer heard of St. Leger's advance on Fort Stanwix, he promptly called out the militia, assembled men and supplies at a point some 30 miles downriver from Stanwix, and set out to the beleaguered fort's relief.

Before attacking Fort Stanwix in full force, St. Leger had to attend to his supply and access route. A wagon track had to be cut through the woods before he could bring up his artillery, and here, as along Wood Creek to the east, the rebels had felled trees that must be cut away. While his men were busy with such chores, St. Leger learned of the 800 rebel militiamen only ten miles away and marching to the relief of Fort Stanwix.

St. Leger was in an unenviable position. He had only 250 regulars available (most of them were to the rear working on the supply route) and his Indians could not be counted on to hold in a set-piece battle. He realized it could be fatal if Herkimer's force attacked him on one side and the fort's garrison marched out to attack him on the other side. That must be avoided at all costs, so he ordered about 400 of his Indians, supported by some of his loyalist troops, to set an ambush for the rebel relief column and destroy it on the march. Ambush was the kind of fighting the Indians understood. They chose their spot well—a narrow ravine near Oriskany, several miles east of the fort, where Herkimer's men would not have room to deploy.

On the morning of August 6, General Herkimer unwittingly led his men straight into a deadly trap. The Tryon County men—those who survived the murderous first fire—kept their heads and formed a defensive circle, facing outward. Herkimer, wounded in the leg early in the fight, propped himself against a tree, set his pipe between his teeth, took up his gun, and by example gave what help he could.

The Indians eventually tired of the battle. Some of them had been drunk when the fighting began; as the alcohol wore off, the battle seemed less compelling to them. It began to rain, and the Indians finally withdrew, leaving the surviving militia masters of the bloody battlefield. Herkimer's men had lost heavily—perhaps as many as 200 killed, and St. Leger claimed 200 prisoners. Many more had been wounded and Herkimer's force was so weakened that there was no question of continuing to Fort Stanwix. Taking their wounded with them, they retreated eastward.

Meanwhile, the garrison at Fort Stanwix had not been idle—nor as unlucky. Upon learning of Herkimer's approach, Willett led a sortie against the nearest of St. Leger's three camps. Without losing a man, he chased the loyalists and Indians into the woods and then systematically plundered the camp, carefully carrying off the Indians' packs, including their blankets.

Having lost many braves and chiefs in the fight with Herkimer, the Indians of the ambush party returned dispiritedly to camp only to find that all their belongings had been either destroyed or taken. This humiliation, daily emphasized by cold nights spent shivering without their blankets, caused the Indians to begin complaining and brooding over their condition. They were being asked to do all the fighting, they said, and St. Leger had broken his word to them.

St. Leger tried to take advantage of his Indians' ugly mood and capitalize on his victory at Oriskany in order to hasten the fort's surrender. He sent messages to the fort, not only requesting its surrender but threatening that, if it did not yield at once, he would not be able to control his Indians— and the garrison as well as all the inhabitants of the Mohawk valley would be massacred. It was the fiery Willett who replied. He refused to surrender, and defied the besiegers to do their worst. He also warned them that they themselves were responsible for any Indian massacres. As he told the message bearers in no uncertain terms: "The message you have brought is a degrading one for a British officer to send and by no means reputable for a British officer to carry." St. Leger hastened to try to soften the effects of what he had said, but the garrison remained adamant; it would resist to the last man. St. Leger had no choice but to retreat or to start an intensified siege. He ordered his men to start methodical approaches to the fort's walls.

When General Schuyler, at Stillwater, heard the news of the Fort Stanwix siege and Herkimer's defeat, he felt he had no choice but to send out a relief force. Not all his officers agreed; after all, Buryogne was near and the American army was pitifully weak. At one point in the discussion, Schuyler was conscious that some of his officers considered him to be deliberately weakening the army to ensure its defeat. The realization stung, and Schuyler is said to have bitten off the stem of his pipe in the tension of the moment. He controlled his temper, emphasized that his was the sole responsibility, and ordered the relief unit to move westward. Benedict Arnold, the driving force behind the Kennebec march and the battle of Valcour Island, volunteered to lead it. Meanwhile, in order to offer more protection to the main body of his army, Schuyler ordered yet another retreat—some 12 miles southward, from Stillwater to the islands at the mouth of the Mohawk River.

Arnold's relief force consisted of General Ebenezer Learned's brigade of Continentals and about 100 militia. Arnold hoped to rally more militia as he went, but when few came forward, he halted about 30 miles east of Fort Stanwix and wrote back for reinforcements. Then came news that St. Leger was pushing the siege to a climax, advancing ever closer to the fort by means of zigzag trenches. He would soon be in position to run a mine under the fort walls to break them. Arnold knew that he could not afford to wait; so, on the chance of being able to outfox St. Leger, he tried a ruse.

At that time, Arnold's men happened to be holding a condemned prisoner named Hon Yost. Yost, a local half-wit, had lived most of his life among the Indians, who looked upon him with great reverence. The Indians interpreted mental deficiency as a sign of being attuned to the Great Spirit, and consequently set great store on a half-wit's prophecies. Arnold offered Hon Yost his life if he would go to St. Leger and give an exaggerated report of the size of Arnold's expedition.

GENERAL ARNOLD.

General Benedict Arnold. Engraved after a drawing by Pierre du Simitière. Courtesy the New-York Historical Society, New York City.

The episode was planned with care, and the delighted Hon Yost played his role to the hilt. When St. Leger's Indians asked about the size of Arnold's army, Yost pointed vaguely to the thousands of leaves on the trees. The Indians were impressed. They feared Arnold, whom they called the "Heap Fighting Chief." Already in a poor frame of mind, they decided to leave at once. Without them St. Leger was helpless, and nothing he could say could dissuade them. On August 23 St. Leger lifted his siege and began a retreat. So hastily did he move that one poor soldier, sound asleep, was left completely behind.

Arnold marched on to Fort Stanwix, left reinforcements there, and hastened back to the main army on the Hudson. Coming on top of the victory at Bennington, the rout of St. Leger meant that, within the span of less than two weeks, Burgoyne's main army had been dealt a severe rebuff and his secondary thrust had been defeated. The chart of patriot fortunes had hit bottom with Herkimer's defeat. Now, slowly but surely, the upswing had begun. The political balance of both New York and New England would now shift in favor of the patriots, and more help could be expected from the militia.

9. The First Battle of Saratoga

In war, as in all protracted contests, neither side can act perfectly according to plan. Action spurs counteraction, and arriving at an accurate interpretation of a delicate balance between adversaries often turns out to be the key to success. Until he moved into the countryside at Bennington, Burgoyne had control of his campaign. He lost it thereafter, primarily because he had not understood that the same geographical features that made the Hudson–St. Lawrence waterway important to the British made it even more important to the Americans. As his threat to the patriots became more obvious, so their opposition to him became more severe.

So far, General Schuyler had retreated before Burgoyne, obstructing his path as much as possible, but failing to halt him. An impatient Congress, smarting from the Ticonderoga defeat, decided Schuyler's usefulness to the Northern Army was at an end. Schuyler was called to Philadelphia; Horatio Gates was named to succeed him. On August 19, the day the new commander arrived at headquarters at the mouth of the Mohawk, Colonel Henry Dearborn, not given to unnecessary words, recorded in his journal that "Genr^l. Gates takes command of the Northern Army this Day which I think will Put a New face upon our affairs."

A new face did indeed begin to emerge, although in fairness to Schuyler it should be noted that he had laid much of the groundwork that made it possible. The news of the Bennington and Fort Stanwix victories soon arrived, and the army received a boost in morale simultaneous with their new commander. A short while later the army's strength was boosted by the arrival of various Continental detachments sent by General Washington.

Washington had spent the summer trying to determine what General Howe intended to do—move northward up the Hudson or descend on Philadelphia. He knew that Howe and a strong force sailed from New York Harbor on July 23, but that did not convince him. Joint action between Howe and Burgoyne seemed "so probable and of such importance" that, as Washington wrote to Gates a week later: "Howe's in a manner abandoning General Burgoyne is so unaccountable a matter that till I am fully assured it is so, I cannot help casting my eyes continually behind me."[8] Not until August 21, when the British were sighted at the entrance to Chesapeake Bay (on a very time-consuming and roundabout route to Philadelphia), was Washington at last certain that Howe was headed for Philadelphia.

Now, at last, Washington could act with confidence. Enterprise was what the Northern Army needed, and the Continental contingents sent north by Washington were intended to help achieve it. Among them was the corps of elite light infantry led by Colonel Daniel Morgan. Morgan's men carried rifles rather than muskets and were renowned for their shooting skill, which gave rise to fantastic (often exaggerated) tales of their accurate marksmanship. The riflemen, who came from the western frontiers of Pennsylvania, Virginia,

General Daniel Morgan. By Charles Willson Peale. Courtesy the Independence National Historical Park, Philadelphia, Pennsylvania.

and Maryland, wore loose-fitting hunting shirts and were accustomed to fighting in the Indian style. Washington thought they should be a "good counterpoise to the Indians"; he suggested that their arrival on the Hudson be played up, even to the point where it would tend "to magnify numbers."

Morgan's corps was indeed a valuable asset. Yet for all their advantages in skirmish warfare and marksmanship, the rangers were at a disadvantage against men armed with muskets and bayonets. The rifle was more accurate and had a longer range than the musket, but it did not have a bayonet and was appreciably slower to load and fire. In close combat, the rifleman could be killed by his opponent's bayonet in the interval between firing and reloading. To strengthen Morgan's corps of 350 riflemen so they could be used in his battle line, Gates assigned to Morgan an almost equal force of 300 light infantry under Major Henry Dearborn. Armed with muskets and bayonets, Dearborn's men gave the riflemen added protection and strength. Not only did the characteristics of their troops effectively complement each other, but Morgan and Dearborn themselves made an effective team. Morgan, a hot-tempered, emotional frontiersman of Welsh ancestry, was a fighter by instinct. He carried on his back the scars of 500 lashes received for striking back at an officer while serving with the British army during the French and Indian war, and the scar on his face came from a wound by an Indian arrow. Dearborn, by contrast, was quieter, with a reputation for steady determination. He had been studying medicine when the Revolution began, but he joined the army at once. Both Morgan and Dearborn were with Arnold on his march to Quebec in 1775, and after Saratoga both would go on to serve in the south, and later, after independence, in the U.S. Congress. On the Hudson waterway that August of

1777, Morgan and Dearborn and their battle-tried men made the strongest infantry unit either side could boast in the coming trial of strength.

That the crucial trial was near was obvious, and Gates prepared for it in his way. He publicized the Jane McCrea scalping incident and capitalized upon it to encourage the militia to join his army. Gradually they came—some at once because they felt their homes and families were in danger. As the season progressed and the fall harvest was completed, others followed suit. By early September, the arriving militia, together with the return of Arnold and his force from Stanwix, had swelled Gates' army to approximately 7,000 men.

Confident that his army was now a match for Burgoyne's, and having been informed by spies of Burgoyne's supply difficulties, Gates decided to advance to meet the enemy. He moved his army north to Stillwater, and then three miles further north, to a spot where a broad and hilly ridge swung close to the Hudson, hemming in the main road between the bluffs and the river. There was no town there—just a few farms in clearings scattered across the well-wooded ridge, and a tavern built by a man named Bemis on the narrow river plain. Gates ordered his Polish engineer, Colonel Thaddeus Kosciuszko, to lay out a defensive position. The men set to work building earthworks and log barriers. The right end overlooked and dominated the narrow plain beside the Hudson; its center stretched west and north across a farm owned by a man named Neilson; its left turned south and then west to merge with the thick woods beyond. Except for a few cleared fields, the area in front of the position was densely wooded and broken by deep ravines—perfect country for the employment of Morgan's frontier riflemen, and difficult country for Burgoyne to make good use of his artillery and massed infantry formations, whereas the fortifications in the plain and on the heights dominating the plain could stop Burgoyne's advance along the river road. Setting up his headquarter on the heights, Gates settled down to wait for Burgoyne.

Of these detailed American moves, Burgoyne knew nothing. His Indians, on whom he had depended for scouting, had largely deserted by now, and most of his plans had to be made without what the modern soldier would call "vital intelligence." However, Burgoyne did know that the rebel force was strong, and getting stronger all the time as the militia swarmed in. He also knew he could expect little help, if any, from Howe. To advance was hazardous; to remain where he was offered nothing; to retreat would be to acknowledge failure. Burgoyne's orders were to get to Albany, but he also was authorized to "act as exigencies may require." He chose to advance. In all likelihood, he was influenced in this decision by a soldier's sense of duty and honor, as well as by the characteristics of his own personality. Burgoyne was bold and aggressive, a gambler by nature, and a proud and ambitious man. If this campaign succeeded, his reputation and future were secure. If he retreated without an all-out effort at achieving success, he would lose forever his chance at greatness.

On September 13-15, Burgoyne's army broke its communications line to Canada and crossed the Hudson above Saratoga (the present-day Schuylerville) on a bridge of boats. After the entire force was gathered on the west bank of the river, the bridge was dismantled, the boats were loaded with supplies, and the little fleet set to drifting downstream alongside the army. With drums beating and colors flying, the troops marched gaily, southward along the river road. Spirits were high. Burgoyne repeated his confident assertion, "Britons never retreat." He was committed to a "calculated risk." Had it succeeded, he would have been judged one of the great commanders of history.

The road along the west bank followed a narrow grassy plain adjoining the river. Although unpaved, it was the best road Burgoyne had yet found during the campaign. However, it was overlooked on the west by a continuous, steep-sided and wooded ridge, from which the rebels could easily pounce upon Burgoyne's column. Because of this danger, it was necessary to maintain a close and orderly line of march for protection in case of attack. This, plus the necessity to rebuild bridges as they went, meant slow going. On September 15 they made only three miles; the next day, they halted to reconnoiter; the day after, they advanced less than three miles. This brought them within four miles of Gates's position on Bemis Heights, but the dense forests hid each side from the other.

Even though he lacked specific knowledge of Gates's position, Burgoyne could surmise where his adversary was. He decided not to continue along the river road, with his forces concentrated, but to divide them into separate groups. Assigning one regiment to guard the boats and another the baggage, he divided the remainder into three columns. Von Riedesel would lead one, advancing as before along the river road. Burgoyne and Fraser, leading the other two columns, would take a nearby wagon track westward over the bluffs and then turn southward along courses roughly parallel to Von Riedesel's. The two columns would make their way through the wooded hills using any available wagon tracks—there was at least one such track said to lead generally southward to the Neilson farm—and thereby get as close as possible to the rebel positions. The purpose is unclear. Most likely, Burgoyne hoped to turn the American left and avoid a frontal clash on a narrow plain by the river.

On the morning of September 19, after a delay to allow the morning fog to lift, the British columns got underway. The forest soon hid them from each other. Von Riedesel, with eight cannon and 1,100 men, started down the river road. Fraser, with eight cannon and about 2,000 men, in-

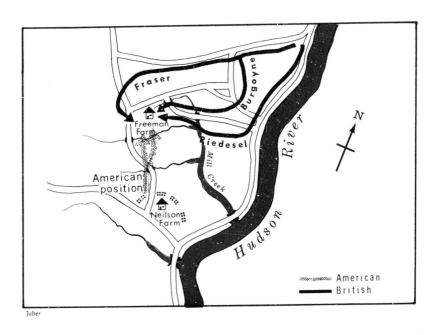

The first battle of Saratoga, September 19, 1777.

cluding the elite grenadiers and light infantry, followed the wagon track inland about three miles and then turned southward. Burgoyne, with six cannon and a force of 1,100 men, followed Fraser for a short distance and then moved southward and westward, aiming for a position roughly in line with and parallel to Fraser's column on his right and Von Riedesel's on his left. The maneuver brought Burgoyne's column to an abandoned 15-acre field that had been cleared by a farmer named Freeman. There, in early afternoon, the British and Americans first made contact. The battle had begun.

The advantage initially lay with the Americans, for, thanks to his efficient scouts, Gates knew considerably more about Burgoyne's moves than Burgoyne did about his. On the morning of September 19, Gates knew the British were advancing toward Bemis Heights through the woods, and he was inclined to wait behind his fortifications for the enemy to approach. Benedict Arnold, however, who commanded the left end of the American position, reasoned that the forest would handicap the British more than the Americans, since it would deny them the full use of their artillery and make it more difficult for them to employ their close-order formations. He urged Gates to move out to meet the enemy. Accordingly, Gates sent Morgan and his riflemen, supported by Dearborn's light infantry, to reconnoiter the enemy's position. The better to search, Morgan divided his men into small groups, and one group bumped into Burgoyne's advance guard at the farmhouse in Isaac Freeman's clearing. Taking the British completely by surprise with their first volley, Morgan's men nearly destroyed the British pickets, or forward scouts. Hurriedly pressing their advantage, they pursued the survivors across the field, but then ran into the main body of Burgoyne's column. The Americans broke and scattered back into the woods. Seeing his men in such confusion, Morgan gasped in dismay, "I am ruined, by God! . . . My men are scattered, God knows where!"

Burgoyne formed three of his regiments, reinforced by part of Fraser's column, into battle line and began to advance across Freeman's field. As they neared the woods on the other side, they were met by the massed fire of a Continental regiment which had just reached the front. The Continentals fired a volley and charged, but the British held firm and the Americans soon faltered and fell back. Other American regiments—plus Morgan's corps—eventually participated in the battle, each in turn falling in on the American left.

As more and more troops became engaged in the fighting, a pattern began to develop. The Americans would fire and charge across the clearing, but time and again they broke before the disciplined British formations and cannon and retreated, pursued by the redcoats, back across the clearing to the woods. There, taking advantage of cover, they repeatedly beat back the British attacks and then counterattacked in turn. The battle swayed back and forth across Freeman's field. Neither side could gain an advantage because neither could stay long enough in the clearing, exposed to the fire of an enemy sheltered by the woods. The woods surrounding Freeman's field kept the battle reasonably restricted. Burgoyne employed three regiments for his battle line. Another regiment posted on his right, plus Fraser's column a little farther to his right, played almost no role in the fighting.

The fire was intense—and deadly. Roger Lamb, a British sergeant, later wrote, "The conflict was dreadful; for four hours a constant blaze of fire was kept up. . . . Men, and particularly officers, dropped every moment on each side. Several of the Americans placed themselves in high trees, and as often as they could distinguish a British officer's uniform, took him off by deliberately aiming at his person. . . ."

The American sharpshooters were mostly Daniel Morgan's rangers. After that first confused clash, Morgan had used his unusual but effective wild turkey call, a small conical horn that imitated the turkey's gobble, to reassemble his men. Reorganized, the riflemen deployed in a thin skirmish line, taking cover behind and in trees and aiming their fire at individual targets. Their ability and usefulness clearly impressed Burgoyne, who wrote that they "hovered upon the flanks in small detachments, and were very expert in securing themselves and in shifting their ground." The casualty figures for the battle also confirmed Burgoyne's opinion: two-thirds of Burgoyne's total losses that day occurred in the ranks opposite Morgan's and Dearborn's men. Especially hard hit were the British artillerymen, who twice had to abandon their guns because of the riflemen's accurate fire; even in the heat of battle, though, the gunners took their linstocks (used to fire the cannon) with them so the rebels could not turn the guns against them. Of the total of 48 artillerymen attached to the center column, 36 were killed or wounded. Lieutenant Hadden, in charge of two guns posted with the Sixty-second Regiment, quickly lost 19 out of 22 men, at which point he went back for aid. He was given more men, but when they returned to the guns, they found that, in Hadden's words, the Sixty-second Regiment "had begun to get into confusion," leaving the guns fully exposed to enemy fire. Hadden's new gunners were soon all wounded, and Hadden lost his guns as the hill on which they were posted was abandoned.

Gradually all the British field pieces, lacking gunners or ammunition, fell silent. American units were threatening to outflank the right of the British line which began to bend back, leaving the center dreadfully exposed. As pressure mounted, the line wavered and seemed about to break. Perhaps it would crumple under the next American charge.

At that desperate moment, much as he had done at

Hubbardton, General Von Riedesel, the stalwart German, marched onto Freeman's field at the head of 500 men and an artillery detachment. Captain Pausch, who was in command of the two 6-pounders, quickly trained his guns on the enemy and in his words, "fired twelve or fourteen shots in quick succession into the foe who were within good pistol shot distance. . . . Presently, the enemy's fire, though very lively at one time, suddenly ceased."

The Germans had struck the Americans' unprotected right flank, with telling effect. Gradually, keeping order and taking many of their wounded with them, the Americans withdrew. It was getting dark. The British and Germans held their fire, but kept a wary eye on the dark woods beyond the clearing. The battle of September 19, the first battle of Saratoga, was over.

Who won? Burgoyne held the field of battle, for what it was worth, so he could claim a tactical victory. In a letter written on the following day, he said: "We have had a smart and very honorable action, and are now encamped in front of the field, which must demonstrate our victory beyond the power of even an American news-writer to explain away."[9]

In the broader sense, the British suffered a serious defeat. Strategically the day was an American victory: Burgoyne had been trying to reach Albany as quickly as possible; he had now been brought to a complete halt by Gates. Not only had the Americans stopped Burgoyne, but they had done so with only 300 casualties as opposed to nearly 600 casualties for the British. Added to the casualties of Hubbardton, Bennington, and Fort Stanwix, Burgoyne's losses at Freeman's farm seemed to confirm the fears of Britain's Adjutant General Harvey that a British army in America might well "be destroyed by damned driblets," because "America is an ugly job . . . a damned affair indeed."[10]

Yet Gates' victory has been criticized on the grounds that he settled for much less than he could have obtained. Gates employed only a fraction of his men, mostly Continentals from the left wing, Arnold's division, of his line. The remainder of the Continentals, plus the sizable body of militia, merely held the Bemis Heights position. They did not move out to destroy the weakly guarded British supplies in the river plain or to encircle Burgoyne or Fraser. Although Learned's brigade did march to meet Fraser's column, it went astray in the woods and made little contribution to the battle.

Unlike Burgoyne, who was in the thick of the fighting, Gates stayed in the rear, and it seems likely that the Americans fighting in Freeman's field had no overall field command. Although some scholars believe Arnold exercised field command on September 19, others find no conclusive proof that he did so. Gates had fought a "safe" battle; and even if Burgoyne was not destroyed, he was severely weakened.

When he heard the news of September 19, General Washington ordered all troops paraded and a gill of rum issued for each man. Now, at last, he was confident that America could count on the "total ruin of Burgoyne." Henry Dearborn was another who was not at all troubled that Burgoyne still held the battlefield. Writing in his journal on the night of September 19, he noted that "we who had Something more at Stake than fighting for six Pence Pr Day kept our ground til Night, Closed the scene, & then Both Parties Retire'd. . . . I trust we have Convinced the British Butchers that the Cowardly yankees Can & when there is a Call for it, will, fight—."

10. *A Tense Interlude*

FOR 16 DAYS following the violent battle of September 19, the forests and fields along the upper Hudson around Saratoga were strangely hushed. Small parties of skirmishers clashed, from time to time, with the advantage generally going to the Americans, who harassed their enemies with glee and determination. Neither side, however, sought to precipitate a showdown.

Gates, for his part, judged his best course was to continue waiting behind the Bemis Heights fortifications. His forces were increasing daily, as more and more militia joined his ranks, while those of his adversary could only get weaker with each passing day. Gates knew that Burgoyne would eventually have to make a move—he could not stay where he was, and he must either retreat or try to force Gates out of his way.

Had Burgoyne attacked the Bemis Heights positions on the day after the first battle of Saratoga, he would have found the Americans short of ammunition, disorganized, and exhausted from their efforts of the previous day. Fortunately for the rebels, however, the British also felt the need of a delay to rest, reorganize, and bury their dead. Unbeknownst to

Gates, Burgoyne did plan to attack again on the day after that, September 21, but that attack was postponed because, shortly before dawn that day, a message arrived from General Henry Clinton that drastically altered Burgoyne's thinking.

Until this time, Burgoyne had pursued his course alone, confident and proud, apparently indifferent to the activities of Generals Howe and Clinton to the south. Now, with failure a sobering possibility, Burgoyne grasped at a feeble hope offered by Clinton.

When Howe headed for Philadelphia with the bulk of his army in July, he left Clinton in New York with only a few thousand troops. His mission was to protect the city, but also, if expected reinforcements arrived from Europe, and he felt able to manage it, to move up the Hudson to support Burgoyne. This meant fighting his way past the rebel army just north of New York, as well as providing for continued protection of the city itself. Clinton thought Howe's move toward Philadelphia was a mistake; as he later wrote: "There was not, I believe, a man in the army except Lord Cornwallis and General Grant, who did not reprobate the move to the southward and see the necessity of a cooperation with General Burgoyne."[11]

There was little communication between Clinton and Burgoyne, not only because news traveled slowly but because most of their messengers were caught and executed by the rebels. Throughout most of the summer, Clinton thought Burgoyne's campaign was moving well. Not until the second week of September did he learn that Burgoyne was not at Albany, as expected, but still 40 miles to the north, at a place called Saratoga. Deciding Burgoyne needed a "little diversion," he wrote on September 12: "You know my good will and are not ignorant of my poverty. If you think 2000 men can assist you effectually, I will make a push at Montgomery [Fort Montgomery, in the Hudson Highlands] in about ten days. . . . I expect reënforcement every day. Let me know what you would wish."

Clinton's letter, one of the few to get through, reached its destination nine days later. Although not offering a great deal of help, it did prompt Burgoyne to call off his planned attack, entrench his men, and await developments. Burgoyne did not stop to think that, in military affairs, it is often fatal to despise one's enemy. To Burgoyne's thinking, should Gates "be rash and ignorant enough" to weaken his army at Bemis Heights and send forces south against Clinton, "he will give me very fair game." Burgoyne wrote Clinton that an attack, or even a threat, on the Hudson Highlands "must be of great use," and he closed by urging Clinton to "Do it, my dear friend, directly."

Burgoyne then ordered his men to dig in and fortify their positions. They constructed a line of defensive fortifications between the Hudson and Freeman's farm, roughly a mile from the corresponding rebel lines. On the bluffs overlooking the river, they built a fortified defensive position, the Great Redoubt, to cover their hospital, the anchored boats, and the pile of baggage and stores. The center of the fortified line (which was not continuous) was at the edge of Freeman's field, a strong position built of dirt-covered log walls 12 to 15 feet high. Outside the walls was an abatis—felled trees with sharpened branches pointing in the direction of attack. Facing south and west, and including the Freeman farmhouse, this position was under the command of the Earl of Balcarres and was called the Balcarres Redoubt. To protect the right flank of the Balcarres Redoubt, another fortification was built to the north and west. Manned by Colonel Breymann's corps, it was called the Breymann Redoubt. Between

(See next page)

Illustration from B. J. Lossing's *Pictorial Field Book of the Revolution,* (1851) vol. I, p. 46. Lossing visited the important sites of the Revolution and sketched them as they appeared around 1850. Reproduction courtesy Ken Perry. **Top of page:** The Neilson farmhouse. The smaller portion on the right is the original house that was standing in 1777. The small outbuilding to the left is on the site of an old log barn that was incorporated into the American lines. **Second from top, right:** The house where Gates had his headquarters during the October 7 battle. **Third from top, right:** The main room in the Neilson farmhouse. **Map:** The battleground for the two battles of Saratoga. **Bottom of page:** View of the Hudson River from Bemis' Tavern. **Left margin:** A halberd plowed up in the area years after the Saratoga battles.

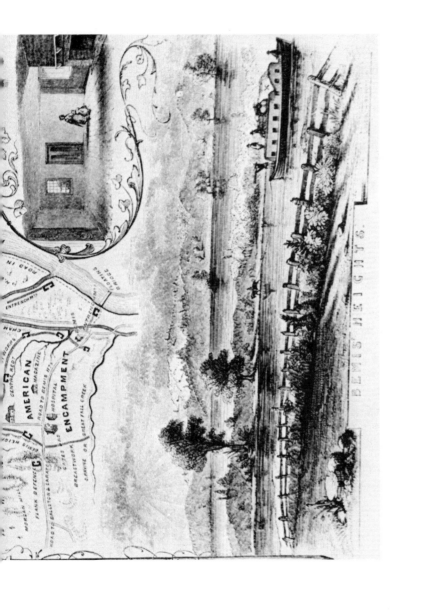

BEMIS HEIGHTS.

the two fortifications, there was a slight draw, where a group of Canadian troops was posted in two stockaded cabins.

Burgoyne's forces settled down—or attempted to—behind their new lines, but they were beset with difficulties. Subjected to a rambunctious harassment by the rebels, particularly by snipers and nighttime patrols, they slept, if they slept at all, fully dressed and with muskets in easy reach. Packs of wolves came down from the Adirondacks to scratch up the shallow graves of the slain, and their howling added to the tension. The nights were cold, the men had no winter clothing and the mornings, when the men were roused an hour before daybreak, were chill and foggy. Rations were monotonous and getting scarce; on October 3 they were cut. The sick rate increased. Desertions rose; hangings did not stop the steady exodus.

Disciplined to hardship and duty, the European regulars maintained surprisingly good morale. Burgoyne himself also seems to have remained confident and optimistic, even after he learned that the Americans had attacked Ticonderoga on September 18. The fort had held, but a number of American prisoners had been released. More than anything else, the incident emphasized that Burgoyne was essentially isolated in hostile country.

In the American camp, by contrast, the overall situation appeared to improve with each passing day. Supplies were plentiful, the position was strong, and the militia continued to come in. Through deserters and his patrols, Gates knew that Burgoyne's army grew weaker daily, both in supplies and men. Gates also knew that Burgoyne counted on Sir Henry Clinton being able to force the Hudson Highlands. Gates, however, was confident that Clinton's attempt would fail and that his own army would be able to direct its full attention to crushing the northern invasion force. Anticipating Burgoyne's retreat, Gates began posting bodies of militia on the east bank of the Hudson to trap the British army. A noose was gradually being draped around Saratoga.

There was nothing dramatic about these preparations, but then Horatio Gates was not a dramatic leader. He came in for criticism, perhaps justifiably, because of his lack of spirited aggressiveness. At one low point in the northern campaign, John Adams fervently prayed "Oh, Heaven! grant Us one great Soul!" and recorded in his diary the despairing judgment that Gates "seems to be acting the same timorous, defensive Part which has involved us in so many Disasters." Yet Gates was in a strong position at Bemis Heights, and he held several advantages. The most important of these, perhaps, was that he had accurately assessed his adversary; he was confident that "the Gen'l designs to resque all upon one rash stroke." Gates may not have been a dashing figure or inspiring leader, but he was nobody's fool. He knew he had only to wait.

The only blot on an otherwise satisfying picture was a rift between Gates and Arnold that did credit to neither. Petty and childish, the argument was in many ways typical of the factionalism and uncemented loyalties that disrupted the American high command throughout much of the war.

There is no doubt that Arnold was a spirited fighting leader, who inspired his men by direct example; one soldier characterized him by saying "It was 'Come on boys'—it wasn't 'Go, boys'." Arnold gave much to the patriot cause, but eventually he turned traitor and was willing to fight just as vigorously for the British. For that reason, any assessment of the man and his role at Saratoga becomes entangled in loyalties and charged with emotion. The truth is elusive, for accounts differ and scholars are still divided on the question of whether or not Arnold participated, other than from a rear command position, in the battle of September 19. In any event, when Gates reported the battle to the Congress he neither mentioned Arnold by name nor identified the units that had fought as Arnold's division. Instead, Gates gave credit to the entire army.

Arnold complained, angrily, and he went so far as to ask for permission to leave the Northern Department and go to Philadelphia to serve under Washington. Gates agreed, but Arnold refused to let the argument die. The issue was further beclouded by the old rivalry between Gates and Schuyler, as well as by the New York-New England factionalism that had beset the colonies long before the Revolution broke out. It was easy for those who supported Schuyler to interpret Gates' action as jealousy of the honor that should have been accorded to Arnold. The other officers at Bemis Heights began to take sides, some supporting Arnold, others seeking reconciliation. Gates met the challenge by transferring Arnold's division to his own command. Bested for the moment, Arnold nevertheless remained in camp—a general with no men to command and nothing to do.

By early October, Burgoyne's sense of isolation had been greatly increased by the press of circumstances. St. Leger, after retreating back to Canada, had indicated he would try to bring his men south by way of Ticonderoga, but he did not come. Neither had Burgoyne heard from Clinton. Actually, Clinton got underway on October 3 and pushed up the Hudson. Making effective use of his 3,000-man force, Clinton captured Fort Montgomery and Fort Clinton on October 6 and thereby broke the rebels' hold on the Hudson Highlands. His force was too small, however, to attempt a thrust all the way to Albany, 100 miles farther north. Although a smaller force continued to press up the Hudson, Clinton seemed to feel he had done about all he could. On October 8 he wrote to Burgoyne that he hoped his "little success" might facilitate operations at Saratoga. Unbeknownst to Clinton, by that time Burgoyne was already defeated. He never received Clinton's message.

On October 4 Burgoyne held his first council of war, in which he was joined by generals Phillips, Von Riedesel, and Fraser. Heretofore Burgoyne had felt confident enough to make his own decisions, but now he felt in need of advice —or else in need of a way to spread the blame in case of failure. The four generals considered the advancing winter and the shortage of supplies. They considered Gates' mounting superiority in men, now estimated at four to one. They bemoaned their own ignorance of the details of their enemy's position; although only about a mile separated them from the rebel lines, the thick woods and undergrowth, combined with vigorous American sharpshooting and patrolling, had prevented much useful reconnaissance.

What to do? Burgoyne had a plan, one that reflected the gambling nature of the man Gates had sized up as an "Old Gamester"; now Burgoyne proposed the "rash stroke" Gates was waiting for. Burgoyne suggested leaving only 800 men to guard the river bank and stores while the rest of the army, some 4,000 strong, would march through the woods to hit Gates' left and rear. His listeners were wary. They pointed out that it might take three days to work their way through the woods to the proper positions; meanwhile the Americans could easily overwhelm the 800 left behind, and that would be disastrous. No decision was reached.

The council convened again on October 5. By then further consideration of their situation had convinced Von Riedesel that Burgoyne's plan was folly. He flatly proposed they

retreat to the east bank of the Hudson, to their position before September 15; there they could await news from Clinton,
and their retreat route would be more secure.

Fraser agreed with Von Riedesel. Phillips kept silent.
Burgoyne rejected retreat as disgraceful and proposed an
alternative plan. With a smaller force—1,500 regulars and
the Canadian and loyalist auxiliaries—he would probe the
left of the enemy's lines on October 7. If this reconnaissance
showed an area of weakness, he would attack with the entire
army on October 8; if it did not, the army would retreat on
October 11, as Von Riedesel had recommended. His generals consented. The time for a final reckoning had come.

11. The Second Battle of Saratoga

LATE IN THE MORNING OF October 7, Generals Burgoyne, Fraser, Von Riedesel, and Phillips led the scheduled "reconnaissance in force" southwestward toward the rebels' left wing. The expedition was composed of 1,500 men and ten artillery pieces—six 6-pounders, two howitzers, and two 12-pounders. Some of the artillerymen thought this was foolish, for, in such terrain, artillery slowed the advance, because it necessitated frequent halts to bridge gullies or rough ground. As one artillery officer insisted, once a 12-pounder moved out into the American woods, it was simply gone.

About two-thirds of a mile southwest of Freeman's farm, the force halted on a gentle swell of land lying north of the ravine through which Mill Creek flowed to the Hudson. They deployed into battle line at the edge of a wheat field. On the right was Fraser with the Twenty-fourth Regiment, plus the light infantry under Major the Earl of Balcarres. Von Riedesel, with the Germans, including Breymann's grenadiers, held the center; the British grenadiers made up the left. The left, abutting on a patch of woods, was near the north-south wagon track leading to Neilson's farm; the right was some 1,000 yards away, anchored in the thick woods to the west.

The wheat field offered open ground for conventional tactics and the use of artillery, but the woods on both flanks offered cover for advancing American forces. It was a vulnerable position. While some of the men began to forage in the wheat field (British horses were also suffering from shortage of food), the generals climbed onto the roof of a deserted log cabin, hoping to see the rebel lines. They saw nothing.

The Americans saw appreciably more. An outpost at Mill Creek quickly reported Burgoyne's move, and Gates sent his ambitious young colonel, James Wilkinson, to reconnoiter. Reporting his observations to Gates, Wilkinson suggested, "I think Sir, they offer you battle."

"What is the nature of the ground, and what your opinion?" replied Gates.

The young Wilkinson did not hesitate. "Their front is open, and their flanks rest on woods, under cover of which they may be attacked; their right is skirted by a lofty height. I would indulge them."

Gates had waited for this moment. "Well, then, order on Morgan to begin the game."[12]

Gates agreed to Morgan's proposal to move through the woods to turn the British right flank from the west. Brigadier General Enoch Poor's brigade was to hit the enemy's left flank on the east; Ebenezer Learned's brigade would hit the center. In accordance with this plan—similar to the three-pronged assault plan Stark had used at Bennington—the three contingents moved into position.

Poor's brigade opened the assault against the grenadiers of the British left. Poor's was a battle-tested brigade of Continentals, and Poor was coolly professional. He ordered his men to take the enemy's first fire, and, after most of it went harmlessly over their heads (a common occurrence when firing downhill), the Continentals unloosed a volley and counterattacked. Captain Pausch, in command of two 6-pound cannon posted at the front between the English and the Germans, wrote that the Americans "advanced madly and blindly in the face of a furious fire."

The Americans reached the height of the small rise where the grenadier lines had originally formed. Some of the British artillery pieces were seized; Colonel Cilley, commander of the First New Hampshire Regiment, jumped astride one of the 12-pounders and ordered it turned around to fire on the British. The grenadiers, outnumbered and outfought,

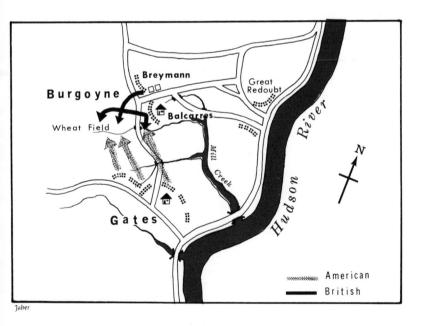

Jaber

The second battle of Saratoga, October 7, 1777.

began to fall back, but it was not a rout. They fought every step of the way. Coming upon the scene later, Wilkinson saw that "in the square space of twelve or fifteen yards lay eighteen grenadiers in the agonies of death, and three officers propped up against stumps of trees, two of them mortally wounded, bleeding, and almost speechless."

Meanwhile, Morgan's assault was developing on the west, as his riflemen moved in against the British light infantry. Before Balcarres could wheel to meet the flank attack, Dearborn's musketmen fired such an effective volley that the British were thrown into disorder. While Balcarres sought to rally his men behind a rail fence slightly to the rear, Learned's brigade joined the fray, advancing strongly against the Germans trying to hold Burgoyne's center. Although both their flanks were uncovered, Von Riedesel's men fought with determination, and their line held. At this point Benedict Arnold galloped into the battle. He did so against Gates' orders, and he had no official command. He seemed like a demon possessed, and later, some observers claimed he had been either drunk or under the influence of opium. But as one historian has suggested, "Neither explanation recognizes the explosive force of thwarted vanity."[13] In any event, Arnold threw himself into the fighting as a self-appointed field commander; Gates remained in his rear headquarters throughout the battle. Although there is controversy over the exact circumstances of Arnold's participation, there is evidence that his spirited entry on the field had a positive effect on the militia. Less highly trained and disciplined than the Continentals, the militia responded well to Arnold's dramatic leadership. And on October 7, unlike September 19, Gates actively employed his militia. He committed to the battle perhaps as many as 9,000 men, of whom approximately 3,000 were Continentals.

Reaching the head of Learned's brigade, Arnold waved his sword and shouted encouragement to rally the men and then led them in another assault on the resisting Germans. Meanwhile, to Arnold's left, Morgan and Dearborn's men were trying to finish off Burgoyne's right wing. General Fraser tried to rally the Twenty-fourth Regiment to cover the British retreat. When Fraser, a conspicuous figure on a fine gray horse, was mortally wounded by an American rifleman, his soldiers lost heart, for Fraser was an able and respected officer.[14] Taking their stricken general with them, the survivors retreated northwestward, along with the Germans of the center and the few remaining Grenadiers of the left. Captain Pausch described the men as "running pell-mell," and tersely noted that many took "early 'leg-bail'." They made haste to reach the protection of the Balcarres and Breymann redoubts.

So far, the action had lasted less than an hour, but the British had already lost eight of their ten cannon and approximately 400 of their 1,500 men. If Burgoyne hoped that the fortifications would enable the remainder to hold and bring an end to the battle, his hopes were soon dashed. The Americans were in no mood to quit. They pressed forward in hot pursuit, reinforced by Brigadier General Abram Ten Broek and his Albany County militia, 3,000 strong, who had just come up from the rear. Learned's and Poor's brigades swarmed through a patch of woods toward the Balcarres Redoubt on a low knoll in Freeman's field.

Arnold led some of Learned's troops in a frontal assault on the Balcarres Redoubt. With its high log walls and outer abatis, the redoubt was a strong defensive position, from which the British could effectively bring their muskets and cannon to bear on the advancing Americans. Repulsed, the attackers took what shelter they could behind trees and stumps, and then continued to exchange fire with the redoubt's defenders.

Leaving them so engaged, Arnold galloped off to the left, riding furiously between the opposing lines of fire, to see what could be done against the Breymann Redoubt. Joining a regiment from Learned's brigade, Arnold led them in a spirited attack on the two stockaded log cabins in the draw between the redoubts. The Canadian defenders quickly gave way, thereby exposing Breymann's left flank. Capitalizing upon this advantage, Arnold led a vicious assault on the redoubt; he led the attack on Breymann's rear while other troops attacked from the front. Breymann himself tried to hold the position, but he was shot by one of his own men and thereafter his men gave way. As a parting gesture they fired a volley and Arnold fell, wounded again in the leg that had been hit at Quebec.[15]

The fall of the Breymann Redoubt ended all hopes that Burgoyne could make an effective stand. Indeed, had it not come so late in the day, his army might have been completely destroyed that afternoon. Oncoming darkness added to the growing confusion of the battlefield, and the Americans decided not to press their advantage right away. Now that they occupied the Breymann Redoubt, they could bolster the captured cannon with their own field pieces and have every confidence of taking the nearby Balcarres Redoubt the next morning.

Burgoyne, realizing he would not be able to hold the redoubt, ordered its evacuation. That night, its defenders quietly moved eastward to join the rest of the army at the Great Redoubt, thereby leaving all of Freeman's farm to the rebels. Burgoyne's gamble had failed. His army had received another morale-shattering defeat. Where Gates' total casualties had been only some 150 men, Burgoyne had lost four times that many—250 in prisoners alone. Burgoyne now had no choice; he must retreat.

12. Retreat and Surrender

DURING THE DAYLIGHT HOURS of October 8, Burgoyne's troops devoted their time to making discreet preparations for their nighttime departure, keeping a wary eye on the rebel lines, and resting as much as possible. At dusk, General Fraser, who had died of his wounds in the morning, was buried, as he had requested, in the Great Redoubt overlooking the Hudson. Several hours after the brief funeral service, the once-proud invaders began the dismal march north.

If there was a sense of desperation about starting back, there was no haste. Although he left behind the hospital with upwards of 400 sick and wounded, Burgoyne was not willing to abandon the remaining artillery, and he could not abandon the stores. Guns and heavily laden carts and wagons pulled by underfed horses meant a slow march; but then it had to be slow anyway to avoid leaving behind the fully loaded boats being rowed upstream against the current.

During the night of October 8, it began to rain—a hard, steady rain that turned the river road into a sea of mud. Burgoyne called a halt, much to Von Riedesel's distress, and the army did not really get underway again until late the next afternoon. It was in the evening that they reached Saratoga, where they had crossed the Hudson so eagerly a month before. Now, while Burgoyne took over General Schuyler's comfortable mansion on the south bank of the Fish Kill, his exhausted men threw themselves down on the muddy ground to rest.

The next morning, Burgoyne moved his entire force across the creek to a safer defensive position, on Saratoga Heights overlooking the Hudson. Before leaving his adversary's estate, though, he ordered the mansion burned down, lest it offer cover to the rebels or obstruct the line of fire of the artillery being emplaced on Saratoga Heights; Burgoyne still had 27 of the 42 cannon with which he had crossed the Hudson in September. The emplacement, the various earthworks erected, and the elevation's command of the open meadowlands below—these gave Burgoyne a strong defensive position, one that would enable his troops to inflict heavy casualties if the rebels tried to storm them.

Following the victory at Bemis Heights on October 7, Gates tended to the needs of his army, allowing his men to take time to draw and prepare their rations for the next few days. On October 10 he assembled his rested forces and pressed northward along the river road to Saratoga. The next two days were spent in positioning troops and cannon, destroying the British bateaux, and seeking to seal off any possible escape route. The noose around Burgoyne was tightening.

By dawn of October 13, the noose was tied. Gates' main body covered Burgoyne to the south; Morgan and Learned were to the west; Stark and some New Hampshire militia were posted on the northwest. Across the Hudson, Brigadier General John Fellows and his Massachusetts militia held a strong position on the east bank, while further to the north

Brigadier General Jacob Bayley and some New Hampshire militia held the road from Fort Edward to Fort George.

While the Americans moved up, Burgoyne had ample time to consider his situation and the alternatives still open to him. Even surrounded, he could perhaps hold his position against attack. But how long would his supplies hold out? Would they last long enough if he decided to wait for Clinton to come to the rescue? Would it be better to pull back to Ticonderoga instead? Again Burgoyne sought help by calling his generals to a council of war. And again it was Von Riedesel who talked bluntly of making a full and swift retreat. He urged abandoning the artillery and baggage; unimpeded, the men could then march quickly northward to a place near Fort Edward, where the Hudson could be forded. Burgoyne vetoed the idea, for he still could not bring himself to abandon his big guns, the prestigious symbol of power. No decision was reached.

Burgoyne's attitude angered not only Von Riedesel but also the German general's wife, a charming and courageous woman who had joined her husband just after what she called "the unfortunate affair at Bennington." Since then, she had shared his hardships and disappointments without complaint, but now she was losing patience with General Burgoyne. Not only did she think he neglected his men, but he seemed inefficient and spineless in not taking more vigorous measures to save his army while there was yet time. Her husband thought retreat was possible if executed at once. Why, then, did they not move? It was in such a mood that she wrote in her journal the passage that, more than any other single commentary, has been linked with the British commander: "Burgoyne liked having a jolly time and spending half the night singing and drinking and amusing himself in the company of the wife of a commissary, who was his mistress and, like him, loved champagne." None could deny that here was a man who enjoyed the pleasures of life. But there was nothing unique about such personal habits; wines, trunks of uniforms, a mistress, and other indulgences were not unusual for an 18th-century general. And it is debatable whether or not Burgoyne's pleasures seriously interfered with his conduct of the campaign. Nevertheless, he may be properly condemned for not realizing the ridiculousness of maintaining such a way of life in a wilderness campaign against a hostile people.

On October 12, though, Burgoyne had to concern himself with grimmer matters. The rebels were moving in all around. Food supplies were dwindling. Time was running out for the British invasion force. Again Burgoyne called a council of his generals.

At this council meeting, Burgoyne outlined five possible courses of action. They could (1) stand pat and wait to see what happened about Clinton; (2) attack; (3) attempt a formal retreat, which would mean taking the guns and baggage; (4) abandon the guns, baggage and boats in order to retreat swiftly by night; and (5) strike suddenly southward toward Albany. Burgoyne and his British officers favored the Albany plan, even though it depended on the Americans moving more of their strength to the west; this might be grasping at straws, but no one ever accused Burgoyne of being a pessimist.

Von Riedesel, who could doubtless see the situation with more objectivity than his British counterparts, argued strongly against the Albany plan. He insisted on the retreat-by-night plan, with the troops taking with them no more than their small arms and whatever provisions they could carry on their backs. The other generals, including Burgoyne, finally concurred. There was a flurry of preparations in the camp, for the retreat was to begin that very night. At the last moment, however, the retreat was cancelled.

Burgoyne's decision came too late. The Americans were now blocking the road north, where Stark had moved into position. The noose was drawn tight.

Burgoyne's situation was grim. His army was surrounded and under siege by a superior force. Furthermore, his men were demoralized, organization was breaking down, desertions were increasing, and the American fire was unrelenting. As for Burgoyne, himself, a man whose personal bravery and courage under fire had never been questioned, he was now, as observed by Lieutenant Anburey, showing anxiety and an agitated bearing. There no longer seemed to be any hope. On October 13, in council with his generals and field officers, Burgoyne decided on surrender.

Had this been inevitable since the arrival at Saratoga? Baroness von Riedesel, who spent those days huddled in a cellar with her three small daughters, answered the question tersely: Burgoyne "could not make up his mind to leave and lost everything by tarrying."

The negotiations for surrender proved to be another kind of war, with each side sparring for the most advantageous terms. The guns remained silent during this engagement as messengers moved back and forth between the two camps.

Gates first demanded what amounted to unconditional surrender. Burgoyne refused. He sent Gates his own proposals, insisting that the British army would surrender only its arms. The men themselves must be allowed to return to England on condition that they would not serve again in America in the present conflict. To the great surprise of all,

the victorious American commander agreed to all the proposals, insisting only that the capitulation be formally signed
by 2 P.M. that same day (October 15) and that the men march
out of their positions by 5 P.M.

Burgoyne was intrigued by Gates' insistence on haste.
Could it mean that Clinton was indeed coming up the Hudson? Was there still a chance to pull victory from the jaws of
this debacle? Ever the optimist, Burgoyne tried finding ex-
cuses for delay. He began haggling over wording—the word
"capitulation" would have to be changed to "convention."
Gates agreed at once.

That night, a loyalist from the south reached Burgoyne's
camp with the news that Sir Henry Clinton had taken the two
rebel forts on the Hudson Highlands and had moved on upriver to Esopus. The informant also reported that since Clinton had reached Esopus eight days earlier, he and his men
were probably in Albany by now. Burgoyne had no way of
knowing that the small force sent upriver from the Highlands
by Clinton would not reach Esopus until October 16 and
never seriously threaten Albany.

On the morning of the 16th, Burgoyne, heartened by
what he thought was accurate news from the loyalist, did what
he could to put off signing the "convention." He accused
Gates of having violated the basis of negotiations by sending
many troops to Albany and thereby lessening the threat of
numbers that had compelled Burgoyne to negotiate in the
first place. He demanded that a delegation of his officers be
allowed to inspect Gates' forces.

Burgoyne's accusation was untrue. It greatly angered
Gates, but its suddenness and harsh tone disconcerted him as
well. Gates, too, had heard that Clinton's force had reached
Esopus; not knowing how strong the British force really was,
he was anxious to conclude the Burgoyne surrender as soon

A transcription of some of the messages exchanged between General Burgoyne and General Gates, as reported in *The PENNSYLVANIA PACKET* for Wednesday, December 17, 1777 (opposite).

The following Messages, &c. passed between Major General GATES and Lieutenant General BURGOYNE, previous to the Convention of Saratoga.

From General Burgoyne to General Gates, October 13, 1777.

LIEUTENANT General Burgoyne is desirous of sending a field officer with a message to Major Gen. Gates, upon a matter of high moment to both armies. The Lieut. Gen. requests to be informed at what hour Gen. Gates will receive him to-morrow morning.

Major General Gates.

General Gates's Reply.

MAJOR Gen. Gates will receive a field officer from Lieut. Gen. Burgoyne, at the advanced post of the army of the United States, at ten o'clock to-morrow morning from whence he will be conducted to head quarters.

Camp at Saratoga, Nine o'clock, P.M. October 13, 1777.

Lieutenant General Burgoyne.

Message delivered by Major Kingston from General Burgoyne to General Gates, October 14, 1777.

I AM directed to represent to you from Gen. Burgoyne that, after having fought you twice, he has waited some days in his present position, determined to try a third conflict against any force you could bring to attack him.

He is apprised of the superiority of your numbers, and the disposition of your troops, to impede his supplies and render his retreat a scene of carnage on both sides. In this situation he is impelled by humanity, and thinks himself justified by established principles and precedents of state and of war, to spare the lives of brave men, upon honourable terms.

Should Major Gen. Gates be inclined to treat upon that idea, Gen. Burgoyne would propose a cessation of arms, during the time necessary to communicate the preliminary terms, by which in any extremity he and his army mean to abide.

General Gates's propositions, with General Burgoyne's reply. October 14, 1777.

1. GENERAL Burgoyne's army being exceedingly reduced by repeated defeats, by desertion, sickness &c. their provisions exhausted, their military stores, tents and baggage taken or destroyed, their retreat cut off, and their camp invested, they can only be allowed to surrender prisoners of war.

. . . .

3. The troops under his Excellency Gen. Burgoyne, will be conducted by the most convenient route to New England, marching by easy marches, and sufficiently provided for by the way.

This article is answered by Gen. Burgoyne's first proposal, which is here annexed.

4. The officers will be admitted on parole, may wear their side arms and will be treated with the liberality customary in Europe, so long as they, by proper behaviour, continue to deserve it; but those who are apprehended having broke their parole (as some British officers have done) must expect to be close confined.

There being no officer in this army under, or capable of being under the description of breaking parole, this article needs no answer.

5. All public stores, artillery, arms, ammunition, carriages, horses, &c. &c. must be delivered to Commissaries appointed to receive them.

All public stores may be delivered, arms excepted.

6. These terms being agreed to and signed, the troops under his Excellency Gen. Burgoyne's command may be drawn up in their encampment, when they will be ordered to ground their arms, and may thereupon be marched over in their way towards Bennington.

This article is inadmissible in any extremity. Sooner than this army will consent to ground their arms in their encampment, they will rush on the enemy, determined to take no quarter.

7. A cessation of arms to continue until sun set, to receive Gen. Burgoyne's answer.

HORATIO GATES.
Camp at Saratoga, Oct. 14, 1777.

Message from General Burgoyne to General Gates, delivered by Major Kingston to Colonel Wilkinson.

IF General Gates does not mean to recede from the first and sixth articles of his proposals, the treaty to end, and hostilities immediately to commence.

General Burgoyne's proposals.

THE annexed answers being given to Major Gen. Gates's proposals, it remains for Lieut. Gen. Burgoyne, and the army under his command, to state the following preliminary articles on their part.

1. The troops to march out of their camp with the honours of war, and the artillery of the intrenchments, which shall be left as hereafter may be regulated.

1. *The troops to march out of their camp with the honours of war, and the artillery of the intrenchments to the verge of the river, where the old fort stood, where their arms and artillery must be left.*

2. A free passage to be granted to this army to Great Britain, upon condition of not serving again in North America during the present contest; and a proper port to be assigned for the entry of transports to receive the troops, whenever Gen. Howe shall so order. 2. *Agreed to, for the port of Boston.*

3. Should any cartel take place, by which this army, or any part of it, may be exchanged, the foregoing article to be void as far as such exchange shall be made. 3. *Agreed.*

4. All officers to retain their carriages, batt horses and other cattle, and no baggage to be molested or searched, the Lieut. Gen. giving his honour that there are no public stores secreted therein: Major Gen. Gates will of course take the necessary measures for the security of this article. 4. *Agreed.*

5. Upon the march the officers are not to be separated from their men, and in quarters the officers are to be lodged according to rank, and are not to be hindered from assembling their men for roll callings and other necessary purposes of regularity.

5. *Agreed to, as far as circumstances will admit.*

9. The foregoing articles are to be considered only as preliminaries for framing a treaty, in the course of which, others may arise to be considered by both parties, for which purpose it is proposed that two officers of each army shall meet and report their deliberations to their respective Generals.

9. *This capitulation to be finished by two o'clock this day, and the troops march from their encampments at five, and be in readiness to move towards Boston to-morrow morning.*

10. Lieut. Gen. Burgoyne will send his Deputy Adjutant Gen. to receive Major Gen. Gates's answer to-morrow morning at ten o'clock.

10. *Complied with.* J. BURGOYNE.
Saratoga, Oct. 14, 1777.

The masthead of the *Pennsylvania Packet*, December 17, 1777, and portion of article giving the surrender terms exchanged by generals Gates and Burgoyne. Reproduction courtesy Fred Hawkins.

as possible. Yet Gates was confident he still held the upper hand, so he sent back a firm reply in which he denied Burgoyne's allegations, turned down the inspection demand—and threatened to break off negotiations. Burgoyne called a final council of all his officers. He tried to persuade them it would be best to continue playing for time, but they all favored capitulation. There was nothing more Burgoyne could do. He yielded to their wishes.

So it was that early the next day, October 17, Colonel Wilkinson led General Burgoyne and his party across the Fish Kill and through the meadow to where General Gates was waiting in the American camp.

The final ceremonies were conducted with dignity and formality. Gates had the British senior officers to a simple but hospitable meal. Meanwhile, Burgoyne's troops marched down to a meadow by the Hudson and stacked their weapons on the ground—a sad ending to the campaign but one that, thanks to Gates' courtesy, was kept out of sight of the victorious army. Later, as the generals of both sides watched the defeated army begin its march south into captivity, Burgoyne followed military custom by turning to Gates and formally surrendering his sword. And Gates, again rising to the occasion, returned it with a courteous bow. It was appropriate that the Revolutionary War campaign that, more than any other, challenged the rigid limitations of 18-century warfare, should end with the protocol of the dying system conducted in the setting of a new concept—that of a nation in arms.

13. The Significance of Saratoga

THE IMMEDIATE EFFECTS of Burgoyne's surrender were to give control of the Hudson–St. Lawrence waterway to the rebel-patriots, to raise their morale, and to increase their incentive for continuing the struggle. But in the long run, the American victory at Saratoga had repercussions that eventually spread far beyond the banks of the Hudson River and the year 1777. Its importance was such that, less than 75 years later, Sir Edward S. Creasy, the foremost English historian of his time, included the battle in his *Fifteen Decisive Battles of the World*. Commenting on Saratoga, Creasy wrote:

> Nor can any military event be said to have exercised more important influence upon the future fortunes of mankind, than the complete defeat of Burgoyne's expedition in 1777; a defeat which rescued the revolted colonists from certain subjection; and which, by inducing the Courts of France and Spain to attack England in their behalf, insured the independence of the United States, and the formation of that transatlantic power which, not only America, but both Europe and Asia, now see and feel.

Modern scholars concur with Creasy that the French

115

alliance brought about by the victory at Saratoga was crucial to the patriots' eventual success. The entry of France and her navy into the war, coming on the top of the failure of the Saratoga campaign, forced Britain to change her strategy for waging war against the Americans; during the remaining years of the Revolution Britain did not again come so close to victory.

Saratoga was not only a turning point in the Revolution itself, but a turning point in the long history of warfare. Saratoga played a significant role in the transition of political and military establishments from 18th-century monarchy to modern democracy; Saratoga stands midway between the 18th century concept of the military as a tool of kings and the modern concept of the military as the embodiment of a nation in arms.

To understand how and why the victory at Saratoga led to intervention by France, it is necessary to go back to the Seven Years War, in which France lost Canada to Britain. Her pride damaged, France bided her time until she could see a favorable opportunity to retaliate against her long-time enemy. The American Revolution seemed to offer that opportunity. The French foreign minister Charles Gravier, Comte de Vergennes, followed developments in America with an eye to intervening in any suitable way to advance the position of France vis-à-vis Britain.

Until it could be seen how capably the American rebels would conduct themselves, France was content to avoid diplomatic entanglements and to offer only material assistance. American privateers and other vessels were allowed to use French ports, both in France proper and in the French West Indies. French officers served with Washington's army. Most important, the French Government secretly financed a private trading firm through which arms and other supplies were funneled to the rebels. Through this company, large quantities of military and commercial supplies flowed westward from France to America during the early years of the Revolution. In the summer of 1777, for instance, France provided 90 percent of the arms and ammunition used by the patriot army facing Burgoyne.[16]

As the fortunes of the rebellion ebbed and flowed, France's interest in greater commitments shifted with them. After the Continental Congress issued the Declaration of Independence in July 1776, for example, the French Government considered an open alliance; but the rebels' defeats at the end of the year dissuaded them. Later, in the summer of 1777, when the French leaders heard of Burgoyne's successes in America and were themselves being pressured by the British Government, they revoked the right of American vessels to use French ports; they were not prepared to go to war with Britain over any lost cause. So Vergennes and his fellow ministers continued to bide their time, while simultaneously strengthening the French navy.

The news of the American victory at Saratoga reached Vergennes on December 4, 1777. Its significance was not lost on the able French foreign minister. This was not a small skirmish, but the defeat of a major British army. It proved the rebels could fight; it also proved that, without the support of the formidable Royal Navy, Britain's armies were not invincible. This, in turn, suggested to Vergennes that France's growing naval support could well be what was needed to enable the American rebels to defeat the British.

Within 48 hours of receiving the news of Saratoga, Vergennes reopened French ports to American vessels and drafted a plan—which Louis XVI promptly and willingly approved —to grant recognition to the rebels and to ally France with them. The actual treaty was signed on February 6, 1778 with the indomitable Benjamin Franklin signing for the United States. With the signing of the treaty, France became the first country to give official diplomatic recognition of the United States of America. In addition to a commercial agreement, the treaty included provisions for a binding political alliance under which each country would neither withdraw until Britain acknowledged America's independence, nor make peace with Britain without the other's consent.

The effects of the French alliance were felt in both America and Europe. Largely through the efforts of Vergennes, Spain and the Netherlands eventually joined France in support of the new nation. Like France, they began by secretly sending aid to the Americans through dummy trading companies. Spain formally entered the war on the side of the United States in 1779, with the Netherlands following suit in 1781. Neither country played a major military role in the war, but their open and official support of the American cause served to bolster the spirits of the American people and encourage the young country's leaders.

It was France, more than any other nation, that militarily helped the United States. And once France, with its powerful navy, became an active participant in the war, the decisive theater became the sea, for control there would determine whether the British could maintain their armies in America. Together with the small but growing navy of the United States, the French navy challenged Britain's long-held supremacy on the Atlantic Ocean—the other great waterway that figured so prominently in the Revolution. French and American ships carried the war to the waters off Britain, as well as America and the West Indies. The maritime struggle dragged on for several years, imposing a constant drain on

Britain's resources and making it increasingly difficult for her to support her far-flung military efforts.

On land, meanwhile, the war entered a new phase after Saratoga, one that could simply be termed "hanging on." The British continued to hold New York; the Americans fortified West Point, in the Hudson Highlands, to prevent a renewed British effort to seize the line of the Hudson. Although Clinton replaced Howe as commander in chief, and Washington maintained the Continental Army in readiness to oppose the new commander, the two adversaries did little more than spar; they did not meet in decisive combat.

Abandoning their initial strategy of isolating New England, the British made an attempt to capture the Southern states. As British forces were not numerous enough to subdue and occupy such a vast and thinly populated region, ultimate success depended on acquiring local loyalist support. Just as had happened along the Hudson—such support failed to materialize in sufficient strength to assure British success. The British armies were soon bogged down in campaigns that accomplished little.

Yet even with the support of France and her other allies, the United States was unable to achieve a quick and decisive victory. The war dragged on into 1781. As the Baroness von Riedesel, still in America, wrote to her mother, "It is a sad war, and it is costing England more than it is worth." Nevertheless, in the spring of that year, Clinton's second-in-command, Lord Cornwallis, who had led the British forces in the South with little long-term success, decided to carry the war into Virginia. Late in the summer, after failing there, too, he moved his army to Yorktown, on a narrow peninsula jutting into lower Chesapeake Bay. This move gave the Americans and French the opportunity they needed. While the French admiral Comte de Grasse used his powerful fleet—superior to any the British could muster to oppose him—to blockade the mouth of Chesapeake Bay, Washington marched 16,000 men, half of them French soldiers, down the peninsula to besiege Yorktown. Cornwallis, with 7,000 men, surrendered after a siege of three weeks. Cornwallis' surrender at Yorktown, four years almost to the day after that of Burgoyne at Saratoga, marked the end of major military operations in America. Almost two years later, a peace treaty was finally signed; the war was over at last, the Revolution had been won.

It is not possible to prove that the Americans would have failed if they had not had an active alliance with France, but there is clear evidence that French aid, particularly naval assistance, played a significant role in the American success. It was largely because of France that Britain was forced to defend herself at sea; that, in turn, prevented Britain from exerting sufficient strength against the American rebels to obtain victory. Conversely, the French alliance brought to the aid of the fledgling United States the superb French navy, a professional French army that made up 50 percent of Washington's strength at Yorktown, and a position in the shifting power of international politics that was diplomatically valuable. The influence of Saratoga stretched far indeed.

In studies of warfare, the American Revolution does not fit easily into the category of the 18th-century limited war, even though it occurred in that century and was fought largely by the military theories and methods typical of the period. But neither does it fit easily into the next chronological category, which is usually called the era of national war. The American struggle is best classified as a transitional war—simultaneously the last of the old regime and the first of the new era.

Most wars of the 18th century were fought by small professional armies. Such an army was customarily the symbol of the country's power, as well as the tool of its ruling class, primarily the monarch. As 18th-century monarchs did not have the power of conscription or of mass taxation, the army was privately raised and financed by the royal treasury. Since an army was expensive to maintain, it tended to be small in proportion to the country's total population and to be employed with discretion to avoid excessive losses of men and equipment. A good general was one who could defeat his enemy through the use of maneuver, bluff, or intimidation rather than bloody battles. It was the era of forts and sieges, of marches and countermarches to obtain strategic advantage, of delays and truces, and when it came down to actual fighting — of formal pitched battles between relatively small armies.

The means of 18th-century warfare were limited partly because the aims were limited as well. Rulers did not seek to destroy each other, but merely to increase their strength or assets at the expense of others. Eighteenth-century limited war was a formal game, bloody and cruel at best, but civilized in comparison to the national wars of the 19th century.

National war, presaged by the American Revolution, ushered in by the French Revolution of 1789, is war involving an entire nation, a nation in arms. The stated goal is often more passionate than practical—liberty, freedom, or some other nonmaterial advantage as opposed to trade or territory. National war affects all of a country's citizens, not merely a small professional army or the ruling elite, for it is based upon the concepts of democracy or participant government rather than the old monarchal system. The concept that every man should have a voice in the government of his country carries with it the corollary that every man must be active in defense of his country. Tax monies finance military establish-

GENERAL BURGOYNE'S SURRENDER*

When Jack, the King's commander bold,
    Was going to his duty,
Through all the crowd he smiled and bow'd
    To ev'ry blooming beauty.
The city rung with feats he'd done,
    In Portugal and Flanders,
And all the town thought he'd be crown'd
    The first of Alexanders.

To Hampton Court he first repairs,
    To kiss great George's hand, sirs,
Then to harangue on state affairs,
    Before he left the land, sirs.
The Lower House sat mute as mouse
    To hear his grand oration;
And all the peers with loudest cheers
    Proclaimed him to the nation.

Then off he went to Canada,
    Next to Ticonderoga,
And quitting those, away he goes,
    Straightway to Saratoga.
With great parade his march he made,
    To gain his wished for station,
When far and wide his minions hied,
    To spread his "Proclamation."

*One of the most delightful ballads of the American Revolution; was sung to a tune still popular today. Reprinted from *Diary of the American Revolution,* (1967), edited by John Anthony Scott; by permission of Washington Square Press, a division of Simon & Schuster, Inc.

To such as stayed he offers made,
    Of "pardon on submission;
But savage bands should waste the lands
    Of all in opposition."
But ah, the cruel fate of war!
    This boasted son of Britain,
When mounting his triumphal car,
    With sudden fear was smitten.

The sons of freedom gathered round,
    His hostile bands confounded,
And when they'd fain have turn'd their back,
    They found themselves surrounded!
In vain they fought, in vain they fled,
    Their chief, humane and tender,
To save the rest, soon thought it best
    His forces to surrender.

Brave St. Clair when he first retired,
    Knew what the fates portended;
And Arnold and heroic Gates,
    His conduct have defended.
Thus may America's brave sons
    With honor be rewarded,
And be the fate of all her foes,
    The same as here recorded.

ments and conscription provides the needed manpower. Compared with limited war, therefore, national war has resulted in, among other things, larger and larger armies, with progressively more bloodshed. Furthermore, since entire nations are involved in such wars, it has become increasingly difficult to bring national wars to an end without the complete overthrow of a nation.

It is in the study of the American Revolution, when the forces of democracy were first giving military expression to a new political concept, that one has the first intimations of the tremendous power of the nation in arms. And it is in the Saratoga campaign specifically that one sees the effects of releasing such power in the fate of the hapless Burgoyne. Saratoga, wrote the modern British historian J.F.C. Fuller, was "the unbottling of the djinn." What Fuller meant is that the American victory at Saratoga would not have occurred without the militia; the militiaman, the citizen-soldier, represents the concept of every citizen a soldier—hence "the nation in arms."

Throughout Burgoyne's campaign, the fortunes of his army rose and fell in direct relationship to the number of Americans who voluntarily took up arms at critical times in the long struggle. True, the Continental Army's regulars provided the steady, continuing core of resistance; without them, the militia units would have had no force to rally around and no way to make their efforts count. Yet the Continental Army was not sufficient in numbers or strength to defeat the British, and it was the numerical boost supplied by the militia that provided the necessary superiority of strength for victory.

Throughout most of the war, General Washington never wavered from the strategic principle that he adopted after his 1776 retreat from Long Island. That principle was to stay on the defensive until the Continental Army could muster a superiority of force. As he wrote to the Congress, "We should on all occasions avoid a general action, or put anything to the risk, unless compelled by a necessity into which we ought never to be drawn." Washington could not and would not risk the Continental Army for the chance of a major victory, no matter how much a victory was needed. If in 1777, such a chance could be taken at Saratoga, it was because the militia gave the Northern Army the necessary superiority of force. In fact, beginning with the Bennington victory in mid-August, it was the militia that tipped the balance in favor of the patriots. Of them, one French officer observed, "When dere be no more militia in dis country, I be one very great Tory [loyalist]."[17]

At the end, Burgoyne's forces numbered somewhere between 4,000 and 5,000 while Gates' Continentals numbered close to 5,000. But the militia swelled the American ranks to approximately 17,000 men—the superiority of force necessary for a decisive action.

In fairness to Burgoyne's troops, it should be remembered that they fought under severe handicaps. They were fighting far from their homes, a circumstance that had an adverse effect on morale. They suffered from shortages of supplies, a condition brought about by the long trans-Atlantic supply route plus the wilderness in which they campaigned. They bore the burden of the strategic shortcomings of their government and their generals, a failure caused by difficult communications plus overconfidence. They also fought in terrain for which their equipment and training were unsuited, and against an adversary that introduced tactics they were poorly equipped to meet. They faced not only a change in battlefield approach, but in the total concept of war, for their enemy was not an army that remained stable in size but a people who rose in arms when danger drew near.

In view of the transitional nature of the American Revolution in the classification of war, and Saratoga's role as the turning point of the Revolution, it is appropriate that Gates used a blend of old and new concepts in this last test. His superiority of force derived from the new phenomenon of a massed citizen-soldiery, but he wielded it with all the skill of a traditional 18th-century general. Although he was criticized for not pursuing his enemy more vigorously in the last days of the Saratoga campaign, he skillfully used maneuver, bluff, and intimidation to accomplish Burgoyne's capitulation without a bloody battle.

It can be said that the concept of the nation in arms was first tried and tested at Saratoga. At Saratoga, wrote historian Fuller, "the sword of Damocles fell, not only on Great Britain, but, because of the fervour of the American Revolution, upon most part of the western world."[18] It is therefore fitting to note that the tune played while Burgoyne's soldiers marched off toward captivity[19] was "Yankee Doodle," a spirited song written by a British surgeon intent upon poking gentle fun at the nonuniformed, unregimented militiaman—who symbolized the political and military era to follow.

Notes

Notes

1. This description of Burgoyne's surrender is based on the eyewitness account of the young American colonel, James Wilkinson, as later set down in his book entitled *Memoirs of My Own Times,* vol. 1, p. 321.

2. A privateer was an armed vessel privately owned, but commissioned by the government to carry on operations of war. The incentive for the privateer was the prize he captured, and his commission, which amounted to a license for piracy, was known as a letter of marque. Between 1775 and 1783 American privateers took about 600 British vessels, including 16 men of war.

3. Bateaux were the standard river and lake craft of the Americas. They were flat-bottomed and built of overlapping planks (lapstraked); they varied in size from 18 to 45 feet.

4. A gondola was a flat-bottomed, square-sailed boat. It was clumsy but strong, and might carry one 12-pound cannon and two 6-pound cannon. A row galley was faster and more maneuverable than the gondola. Probably keeled, it had sails as well as oars. One American row galley captured by the British was described as having an 18-pounder and a 12-pounder in the bow,

two 9-pounders in the stern, and six 6-pounders on broadside. Both gondolas and galleys carried swivel guns as well as cannon. Larger vessels of the period can be identified as follows: a ship was square-rigged with three masts; a schooner was fore-and-aft rigged with two or more masts; a sloop was fore-and-aft rigged with one mast.

5. William L. Stone, *Journal of Captain Pausch,* pp. 82-83.

6. Each British regiment was composed of ten battalion companies plus one company of grenadiers and one company of light infantry. Grenadiers were the tallest and strongest men; they served as shock troops. The light infantry were the best recruits; they served as scouts and skirmishers. The advanced corps was formed by detaching the light infantry and grenadier companies from each regiment and incorporating them into a single unit. In Burgoyne's army, the advanced corps consisted of the flank companies (grenadiers and light infantry) from the Ninth, Twentieth, Twenty-First, Twenty-Fourth, Forty-Seventh, Fifty-Third and Sixty-Second regiments, together with the flank companies from three other regiments retained by Carleton in Canada. The German troops under Burgoyne also employed an advanced corps organization, using a grenadier battalion and a company of light infantry which included 40 jagers (riflemen) and 40 marksmen selected from different regiments.

7. From Burgoyne's letter of June 22, 1777 to General Harvey. *State of the Expedition,* p. xlvii.

8. From Washington's letter of July 30, 1777, to General Gates. Quoted in Freeman, *George Washington,* Vol. 4, pp. 446-47.

9. From Burgoyne's letter of September 20, 1777 to the commander at Ticonderoga. Quoted in Nickerson, *Turning Point of the Revolution,* pp. 316-17.

10. Quoted in Nickerson, *Turning Point of the Revolution,*
    p. 44.

11. From a commentary written by Clinton for a history of
    the Revolution. Cornwallis and Grant were British
    generals; the former is best remembered as the com-
    mander of the army that surrendered at Yorktown in
    1781; Grant commanded an expedition in the French
    West Indies. Quote from Nickerson, *Turning Point of
    the Revolution,* p. 339.

12. The dialogue is taken from Wilkinson's own memoirs,
    Vol. 1, p. 267. However, because portions of his ver-
    sion of the campaign are distorted to give him a dis-
    proportionate share of glory, his entire account must
    be viewed with reserve.

13. John R. Cuneo, *The Battles of Saratoga,* p. 68. New
    York: The Macmillan Company, 1967.

14. General Fraser's death, like that of Jane McCrea, has
    become entangled in legend. It is frequently asserted
    that Morgan ordered one of his marksmen, a certain
    Tim Murphy, to climb a tree and shoot the general.
    And Sergeant Lamb recorded that, before dying the
    following day, Fraser himself told how he had been
    shot by a rifleman in a tree. Another account, written
    by a British prisoner of war who met Morgan in 1781,
    narrates a conversation in which Morgan said (of the
    October 7 battle) that he had observed one enemy
    officer's dynamic leadership and ordered a rifleman
    to climb a tree and eliminate the man. Even so, the
    story of Tim Murphy has not been decisively sub-
    stantiated.

15. Some years later, after Arnold's treason had been ex-
    posed, an American soldier was asked what he thought
    should be done with Arnold—an academic question
    in light of the fact that Arnold was never brought to
    justice. The soldier suggested that Arnold's leg,

wounded twice in the service of his country, could be cut off and given a decent burial. As for the rest of the man, he could be hanged.

16. See Claude H. Van Tyne, "French Aid Before the Alliance of 1778," *American Historical Review,* vol. XXXI (1925), pp. 37-40.

17. From an article in *The Pennsylvania Packet,* Sept. 5, 1778. Quoted in Frank Moore, *Diary of the American Revolution,* 1967 edition, p. 262.

18. J.F.C. Fuller, *A Military History of the Western World.* N.Y.: Funk & Wagnalls Company, Inc., 1955. Vol. 2, p. 309.

19. The British and German troops taken prisoner at Saratoga spent the remainder of the war in America, first at Boston and later in Virginia and Pennsylvania. The American Congress was reluctant to abide by the terms of Gates's convention, which would have allowed the army to return to Britain to release other soldiers for service in America. By various means, the army's return was delayed. Years later, in 1932, it was discovered that General Howe planned to violate the convention terms by transporting the army from Boston directly to New York to join his army.

Bibliography

Bibliography

Contemporary Accounts

Anburey, Thomas. *Travels Through the Interior Parts of America.* 2 vols. First published 1789. Reissued Boston and New York: Houghton Mifflin Co., 1923.

Baxter, James Phinney. *The British Invasion From the North. The Campaigns of General Carleton and Burgoyne, with the Journal of Lieutenant William Digby.* Albany, N.Y.: Joel Munsell's Sons, 1887.

Benians, E. A. (ed.). *A Journal by Thos. Hughes.* New York: Kennikat Press, 1947. [Hughes was a British soldier; his journal is of particular interest for the period of captivity after 1777].

Bradford, Sydney (ed.). "Lord Francis Napier's Journal of the Burgoyne Campaign." *Maryland Historical Magazine,* vol. 57, no. 4 (December 1962).

Brown, Lloyd A. and Peckham, Howard H. (ed.). *Revolutionary War Journals of Henry Dearborn 1775-1783.* Chicago: The Caxton Club, 1939.

Brown, Marvin L., Jr. (Trans. and ed.). *Baroness von Riedesel and the American Revolution.* Williamsburg, Va.: Institute of Early American History and Culture, 1965. [Contains the baroness' journal plus editorial explanations.]

Burgoyne, Lieutenant General John. *A State of the Expedition from Canada.* 2nd ed. London, 1780.

Clark, Jane. "Responsibility for the Failure of the Burgoyne campaign," *American Historical Review,* vol. XXXV (April 1930).

Commager, Henry Steele and Morris, Richard B. (ed.). *The Spirit of 'Seventy-Six.* New York and Indianapolis: The Bobbs-Merrill Co., 1958.

"Diary of Jonathan Pell," *Magazine of American History,* vol. II, (February 1878). [Pell's *Diary* is one of the four published accounts of the campaign, from the British side, and written at the time. The others are Hadden's *Journal,* Burgoyne's *Journal* (in State of the Expedition), and Napier's *Journal.* Accounts by Anburey, Digby, and Lamb were written after the events. These four accounts strongly support each other.]

Hadden, Lieut. James M. *A Journal Kept in Canada and Upon Burgoyne's Campaign, Orderly Books.* Edited by Horatio Rogers. Albany, N.Y.: Joel Munsell's Sons, 1884.

Journal of Bayze Wells of Farmington, May 1775-February 1777. ("Collections of the Connecticut Historical Society," vol. VII.) Hartford: The Society, 1899.

Journal of Oliver Boardman of Middletown. ("Collections of the Connecticut Historical Society," vol. VII.) Hartford: The Society, 1899.

Lamb, Roger. *An Original and Authentic Journal of Occurrences during the late American War, from its Commencement to the year 1783.* First published Dublin, 1809. Reissued New York: Arno Press, 1968.

Moore, Frank. *Diary of the American Revolution.* First published, 2 vols., New York, 1860. Abridged version published New York: Washington Square Press, 1967.

Narrative of Col. Ethan Allen's Captivity, Written by Himself. Burlington, Vt.: Chauncey Goodrich, 1846.

Pettingill, Ray W. (trans.). *Letters from America 1776-1779.* Boston and New York: Houghton Mifflin Co., 1924. [Letters written home by the German troops serving under Burgoyne.]

Roberts, Kenneth. *March to Quebec: Journals of the Members of Arnold's Expedition.* New York: Doubleday, Doran & Co., 1938.

Stark, Caleb. *Memoir and Official Correspondence of Gen. John Stark.* Concord: Edson C. Eastman, 1877.

Stone, William L. (trans. and ed.). *Journal of Captain Pausch.* Albany, N.Y.: Joel Munsell's Sons, 1886.

Wilkinson, General James. *Memoirs of My Own Times.* Vol. 1. Philadelphia, 1816.

General and Biography

Bilias, George Athan (ed.). *George Washington's Generals.* New York: William Morrow and Co., 1964.

————. *George Washington's Opponents.* New York: William Morrow and Co., Inc., 1969.

Creasy, Edward S. *Fifteen Decisive Battles of the World.* First published 1851. Reissue of 2nd ed. Harrisburg, Pa.: Military Service Publishing Co., 1955.

De Fonblanque, Edward Barrington. *Political and Military Episodes in the Latter Half of the Eighteenth Century, Derived from the Life and Correspondence of The Right Honorable John Burgoyne, General, Statesman, Dramatist.* London: Macmillan and Co., 1876.

Flexner, James Thomas. *The Traitor and the Spy.* New York: Harcourt, Brace and Co., 1953. [Biography of Arnold.]

Freeman, Douglas Southall. *George Washington*. Vols. 3, 4. New York: Charles Scribner's Sons, 1951.

Gerlach, Don R. *Philip Schuyler and the American Revolution in New York*. Lincoln: University of Nebraska Press, 1964.

Hargrove, Richard John. "General John Burgoyne 1722-1777." Unpublished Ph.D. dissertation, Department of History, Duke University, 1970.

Higginbotham, Don. *Daniel Morgan, Revolutionary Rifleman*. Chapel Hill: University of North Carolina Press, 1961.

Mackesy, Piers. *The War for America 1775-1783*. Cambridge, Mass.: Harvard University Press, 1965.

Mahan, A. T. *The Major Operations of the Navies in the War of American Independence*. Boston: Little, Brown and Co., 1913.

Nickerson, Hoffman. *The Turning Point of the Revolution*. Boston and New York: Houghton Mifflin Co., 1928.

Partridge, Bellamy. *Sir Billy Howe* [contains *Howe's Narrative*, a brief memoir by General Howe] London: Longmans, Green and Co., 1932.

Patterson, Samuel White. *Horatio Gates, Defender of American Liberties*. New York: Columbia University Press, 1941.

Peterson, Harold L. *The Book of the Continental Soldier*. Harrisburg, Pa.: The Stackpole Co., 1968.

Smith, Justin H. *Our Struggle for the Fourteenth Colony*. New York: G. P. Putnam's Sons, 1907.

Wright, John Womack. *Some Notes on the Continental Army*. Cornwallville, N.Y.: Hope Farm Press, 1963.

Wrong, George M. *Canada and the American Revolution*. First published 1935. Reissued New York: Cooper Square Publishers, 1968.

Index

Index